T0130231

Do You See This Woman?

Six Women Who Encountered Jesus
Face-to-Face

LAYNIE TRAVIS

WESTBOW
PRESS®
A DIVISION OF THOMAS NELSON
& ZONDERVAN

Copyright © 2019 Laynie Travis.

All rights reserved. No part of this book may be used or reproduced by any means, graphic, electronic, or mechanical, including photocopying, recording, taping or by any information storage retrieval system without the written permission of the author except in the case of brief quotations embodied in critical articles and reviews.

WestBow Press books may be ordered through booksellers or by contacting:

WestBow Press
A Division of Thomas Nelson & Zondervan
1663 Liberty Drive
Bloomington, IN 47403
www.westbowpress.com
1 (866) 928-1240

Because of the dynamic nature of the Internet, any web addresses or links contained in this book may have changed since publication and may no longer be valid. The views expressed in this work are solely those of the author and do not necessarily reflect the views of the publisher, and the publisher hereby disclaims any responsibility for them.

Any people depicted in stock imagery provided by Getty Images are models, and such images are being used for illustrative purposes only. Certain stock imagery © Getty Images.

ISBN: 978-1-9736-6909-8 (sc)
ISBN: 978-1-9736-6908-1 (e)

Library of Congress Control Number: 2019910105

Print information available on the last page.

WestBow Press rev. date: 08/02/2019

Scripture quotations marked (NIV) are taken from the Holy Bible, New International Version®, NIV®. Copyright © 1973, 1978, 1984, 2011 by Biblica, Inc.™ Used by permission of Zondervan. All rights reserved worldwide. www.zondervan.com The "NIV" and "New International Version" are trademarks registered in the United States Patent and Trademark Office by Biblica, Inc.™

Scripture quotations marked (KJV) taken from the King James Version of the Bible.

Scripture quotations marked (NKJV) taken from the New King James Version®. Copyright © 1982 by Thomas Nelson. Used by permission. All rights reserved.

Scripture quotations marked (ESV) are from the ESV® Bible (The Holy Bible, English Standard Version®), copyright © 2001 by Crossway Bibles, a publishing ministry of Good News Publishers. Used by permission. All rights reserved.

Scripture quotations marked (NASB) taken from the New American Standard Bible® (NASB), Copyright © 1960, 1962, 1963, 1968, 1971, 1972, 1973, 1975, 1977, 1995 by The Lockman Foundation Used by permission. www.Lockman.org

Scripture quotations marked (NLT) are taken from the Holy Bible, New Living Translation, copyright ©1996, 2004, 2015 by Tyndale House Foundation. Used by permission of Tyndale House Publishers, Inc., Carol Stream, Illinois 60188. All rights reserved.

Scripture quotations marked (CEV) are taken from the Contemporary English Version®, Copyright © 1995 American Bible Society. All rights reserved.

Scripture quotations marked (GNT) are taken from the Good News Translation (GNT) in Today's English Version- Second Edition Copyright © 1992 by American Bible Society. Used by Permission.

Scripture quotations marked (BSB) are taken from The Holy Bible, Berean Study Bible, BSB Copyright ©2016, 2018 by Bible Hub Used by Permission. All Rights Reserved Worldwide.

Scripture quotations marked (MSG) are taken from THE MESSAGE, copyright © 1993, 2002, 2018 by Eugene H. Peterson. Used by permission of NavPress. All rights reserved. Represented by Tyndale House Publishers, Inc.

Laynie Travis is in love with Jesus, her husband, her children, and spreading the good news of the gospel! She was saved at a young age and loves Jesus with all of her heart. While raising her large family, Laynie felt the Lord nudge her to put her faith into action and start a Bible study in her local community. Suddenly, a new passion was born inside of her, and that one faith step has now inspired her to not only teach but also start writing Bible devotionals.

Let's stay in touch!
Visit my website, www.laynietravis.com for updates and please follow me on social media.
Instagram: @laynietravis Facebook: @authorlaynietravis Twitter: @laynietravis

Contents

INTRODUCTION

As a woman, have you ever felt invisible, unheard, or unneeded? Have you ever wondered how Jesus sees you?

In this study, we'll examine face-to-face encounters between Jesus and six different women in the Bible. We'll see that while each of these women faced very different sets of challenges and circumstances, Jesus saw them and gave each of them what they needed.

As we learn their individual stories, we'll discover that they aren't so different from you and me. They experienced many of the same struggles we face today. They suffered heartache, shame, rejection, and isolation. They were misunderstood, marginalized, and stuck in sin cycles they couldn't seem to escape from. These women knew they needed a savior, and Jesus met them in their need.

The powerful encounters these women shared with Jesus left them transformed. He welcomed them right where they were, but He didn't leave them there. Jesus saw their heart, potential, and divine purpose. He showed each of these women the way to a new life and empowered them to live in His freedom—just as He does for us today.

We can easily get can bogged down with the worries and hardships of this world. But like these women, when we meet with Jesus, we find exactly what we're looking for. In a world where we can feel invisible, Jesus gives us a safe place to turn.

Know this: You're not alone. You are loved and desired. Jesus sees you, rescues you, empowers you, frees you, enlightens you, and comforts you with His eternal presence.

About the Study

Join me in the six-week study, and let's discover the transforming power of the God who sees us.

- The first video session is an introduction to the series.
- Each week we'll study individual women who were seen by Jesus.
- In the second and following weeks, we'll gather as a group and dive deeper into her experience with a teaching video followed by group discussion.
- This study is designed to bring women together. I encourage you to find a group or step out in faith and form a group!
- All teaching videos can be found at www.laynietravis.com/doyouseethiswoman
- If you need help or encouragement along the way, please reach out to me at hello@laynietravis.com!

Group Guide

- Welcome the Group
- Open in Prayer
- Watch Introduction video found at laynietravis.com/doyouseethiswoman (27:10)
- Go over discussion questions

1. What are the many "hats" women wear today (e.g., mother, daughter, etc.)?
2. How can your identity get lost in one of these roles?
3. When have you felt invisible?
4. What are some challenges women face in today's culture?
5. How do you think God sees you?
- Close in Prayer

The Woman Jesus Saw (Do You See This Woman?)

Day 1: The Uninvited Guest

Have you ever been to a party you weren't invited to? A handful of times in my life, I can remember going with friends to a lunch or barbeque, even though I wasn't on the text thread or evite. I always arrived feeling insecure and awkward, even if it was just a casual gathering.

Let's take that to another level. Imagine going to a party you weren't invited to and the hosts can't stand you. This makes the scenario way worse. My mom refers to situations like these as walking into the lion's den.

Today, we're going to explore the story of a woman who had every right to feel insecure and even afraid of going to a dinner party. She was considered a social outcast, and the man hosting the dinner wanted nothing to do with her—much less have her show up at his house. Yet in her determination to get to Jesus, she showed up at the party anyway, uninvited and unwanted. I get social anxiety just thinking about that. Just saying.

Read Luke 7:36–50.

According to this Bible story, a Pharisee named Simon invited Jesus to a dinner party at his home. Jesus accepted the invitation, went to the party, and reclined at the table.

In this culture, dinner guests would lie next to the table on couches, prop themselves up on one elbow, and stretch their feet out behind them. It sounds awkward, but this was the table etiquette of the day. (I'm glad we sit up in chairs nowadays. I'm extremely inflexible, and this sounds like the perfect recipe for a neck spasm.)

Read Luke 7:37–38 again.

The Bible points out that this unnamed woman attended the dinner because she learned that Jesus would be there. She heard Jesus was in town at the house of Simon the Pharisee and made it her mission to be at this dinner.

This alone tells us a lot about her. She was brave, and she was passionate about getting close to Jesus. She went to great lengths in pursuit of Him. She was so intent on seeing Him that she broke through the Jewish laws and social norms of the day to show up at a Pharisee's home.

Needless to say, she was not a welcome guest at this party—or any party, for that matter. She would've been a woman of poor repute in her society, and she certainly wouldn't have run in religious elite circles. She would've known that with her reputation, she was taking a huge risk even going to this home. She could've easily been thrown out. She was considered unclean, and the Pharisees would've thought that her presence alone would defile them.

To fully understand the risk this woman took, we need to learn a little more about the Pharisees. Who are they? What were they all about? Let's take a look.

The word *Pharisee* in Hebrew is *Parush,* which means "one who is separated." The Pharisees were an ancient Jewish separatist party of scribes and sages who took their laws to the extreme. Members of this sect believed that to remain "clean" or "holy," they needed to separate completely from people they considered "unclean" or "sinners." They basically thought they were better than everyone else.

"Where did this clean versus unclean principle come from?" you ask. Let's get to the bottom of it with a brief history lesson.

In the Old Testament, God set the Jewish people apart and established the law to show them how to live in a community of peace, holiness, and justice. They served as an example of a God-honoring people to the surrounding pagan nations.

The moral law for the Jewish people included a system to atone for sin, which was done through animal sacrifices. Here's why:

> For all have sinned and fall short of the glory of God. (Romans 3:23 NIV)

> For the life of the creature is in the blood, and I have given it to you to make atonement for yourselves on the altar; it is the blood that makes atonement for one's life. (Leviticus 17:11 NIV)

God takes sin seriously, so to atone for their sins, the Jewish people had to honor these laws. God established them to show humankind that no one is clean. We all sin and need a savior. He gave the Jewish people a system to repent, be washed clean, and return to Him.

This sacrificial system foreshadowed a coming Christ. By becoming the perfect sacrifice on the cross, Jesus fulfilled the old system. When we surrender our lives to Him, we're made clean by His blood, once and for all.

> Do not think that I have come to abolish the Law or the Prophets; I have not come to abolish them but to fulfill them. (Matthew 5:17 NIV)

Now let's look at how the Pharisees play into all of this.

The Pharisees abused the external laws that God established for the Jewish people in the Old Testament by adding laws that were unnecessary and burdensome to people.

Look at what Jesus said about—and directly to—the Pharisees.

> They pile heavy burdens on people's shoulders and won't lift a finger to help. Everything they do is just to show off in front of others. They even make a big show of wearing Scripture verses on their foreheads and arms, and they wear big tassels for everyone to see. (Matthew 23:4–5 CEV)

> You are nothing but snakes and the children of snakes! How can you escape going to hell? (Matthew 23:33 CEV)

Jesus didn't mince words. He's doing more than warning them. He's telling them that they're dead wrong—literally.

The Pharisees turned the law God created to bring peace, restoration, and justice into human-made rules that promoted self-righteousness and religious control. They used religion as a means of manipulation and fear to make themselves appear holy and lord power over others. Rather than leading their people to repent and be forgiven of their sin, they condemned and ostracized them and began to play God.

This is a dangerous place to be. Remember Satan was cast out of heaven for wanting to be like God. (See Isaiah 14:12–14.)

Okay, history lesson over. Let's get back to story of the woman at the party.

To recap, she knew that the Pharisee Simon thought she was unclean and would pollute everyone present. After learning about the culture she was part of, we can appreciate the courage it would take for her to show up there.

Read Luke 7:38 again.

The woman was hiding in the shadows. We can see how she viewed her worth just by where she chose to stand. She knew her place. She knew that she wasn't invited, yet in her desperation, she stood behind Jesus, placing herself at His feet.

She didn't want to draw attention. She only wanted to be near Jesus. She seemed to understand that His opinion was the only one that really mattered and that if she could just get to Him, He'd be able to help her.

There's one more note about this woman. In this passage, she's referred to as an "immoral" or "sinful" woman. We can assume from these references that she was a prostitute. Women were considered second-class citizens at best in this culture, so that alone would be enough to drive insecurity, but this woman was also a prostitute. She would've been the embodiment of shame.

So this woman hid, knowing what everyone at the party would've seen when they saw her. I can't help but wonder if she ever asked herself, *What does Jesus think of me?*

In her desperation, she took a chance on Him, hoping and praying that He welcomed her instead of throwing her out. We can only use our imaginations, but my guess is that she had heard stories of Him healing people and helping people. Maybe she had seen Him teach. Whatever the case, she assumed that she could trust Jesus. And she assumed correctly.

Let's end here for today. What we know so far is that this woman showed great faith and took a massive risk to get to Jesus. Even in her sin and shame, she sought Him out.

Let this be a lesson to us all: Get to Jesus at all costs. We can come to Him in our mess, with our fears, and against all opposition. When we do, we'll always find that He's worth it.

Questions

1. Read Luke 7:36–50. Who was hosting the dinner party for Jesus?
2. According to Luke 7:37–38, who else came to this dinner?
3. What's the Hebrew word for "Pharisee," and what does it mean?
4. Why did Jesus oppose the doctrine of the Pharisees? (See Matthew 23:4–5.)

Day 2: Undone

We left off yesterday with the unnamed woman, known only by her great sin, courageously going to a party she wasn't invited to. She hoped to find Jesus.

Today, let's pick up at the dinner party.

> As she stood behind him at his feet weeping, she began to wet his feet with her tears. Then she wiped them with her hair, kissed them and poured perfume on them. (Luke 7:38 NIV)

Okay, she's standing behind Jesus, weeping and washing His feet with her tears. So much for not drawing attention. She's now making a scene.

I imagine her kneeling at Jesus's feet while sobbing. It seems that when she saw Him, she simply couldn't contain her tears.

There are times in my life when something upsets me, I get in a tiff with my mom, or I butt heads with one of my sisters. Usually, I can compartmentalize those feelings, get over it, and move on with my day. But there are also times when I receive some news (either good or bad) that rocks me to the core. Sometimes, I just can't contain the tears.

I have to say I do cry easily. When it involves my husband or kids, forget about it! Once the tears start flowing, it's hard to make them stop. We've all had those ugly cry moments when we just can't regain our composure, no matter how hard we try.

One of my best friends is worse than me. If you even say the word *college*, she'll burst into tears, thinking about her kids leaving home. We've all been there.

Well, this is where this woman found herself. Here she is at a party she's not even supposed to be attending. She sees Jesus, and she's undone at the mere sight of Him. She can't play it cool or hide her feelings.

Let's look at some other examples of Bible figures who had similar reactions to the sight of Jesus:

In the year that king Uzziah died I saw also the Lord sitting upon a throne, high and lifted up, and his train filled the temple.... And the posts of the door moved at the voice of him that cried, and the house was filled with smoke. Then said I, Woe is me! for I am undone; because I am a man of unclean lips and I dwell in the midst of a people of unclean lips: for mine eyes have seen the king, the Lord of hosts. (Isaiah 6:1, 4–5 KJV)

Jesus, knowing all that was going to happen to him, went out and asked them, "Who is it you want?' "Jesus of Nazareth," they replied. "I am he," Jesus said. (And Judas the traitor was standing there with them.) When Jesus said, "I am he," they drew back and fell to the ground. (John 18:4–6 NIV)

As he journeyed he came near Damascus, and suddenly a light shone around him from heaven. Then he fell to the ground, and heard a voice saying to him, "Saul, Saul, why are you persecuting Me?" And he said, "Who are You, Lord?" Then the Lord said, "I am Jesus, whom you are persecuting. It is hard for you to kick against the goads." So he, trembling and astonished, said, "Lord, what do you want me to do?" (Acts 9:3–6a NJKV)

These are only a few examples of people who lost composure when they saw Christ as Lord. They couldn't stand in His presence without seeing their own sin, and it moved them to a place of surrender. Whether in tears or falling on their knees, they couldn't contain themselves in the presence of His glory.

This is a scary place for us to be, but also a freeing place. The façade is down, and we stop caring about what others think. When we realize that Jesus is Lord, we're undone in His presence.

I believe this is where this woman found herself. She understood who Jesus was more than any of the religious leaders at this party. She saw Jesus as Lord, and she couldn't stop the tears.

Read Luke 7:38 again.

The Bible tells us that this woman cried so much, she was able to wash Jesus's feet with her tears. That's a lot of tears. Words were lost on her. She was swallowed up in emotion.

I love that in her brokenness, insecurity, and low self-worth, this woman felt safe in the presence of Christ. It was as if no one else was there. His presence alone ministered to her. She lavished her great love on Him, returning the love she must have felt from Him.

Note that at this point, Jesus hadn't yet spoken a word to her, yet she wept, kissed His feet, and then poured her perfume on His feet, wiping them with her hair. This is such an intimate act of love and humility. She poured out her heart, her sin, her regret, her tears, and her fear in an act of tender worship. She is the picture of a truly repentant heart.

This scene is one of many examples of Jesus attracting those who need His love and mercy. He's God in the flesh—the very personification of love. We can assume that His gaze and countenance were gentle and welcoming.

Let's read more about Jesus's character:

> The Son is the image of the invisible God, the firstborn over all creation. (Colossians 1:15 NIV)

> But you, O Lord, are a God merciful and gracious, slow to anger and abounding in steadfast love and faithfulness. (Psalm 86:15 ESV)

> The Lord your God is in your midst, a mighty one who will save; he will rejoice over you with gladness; he will quiet you by his love; he will exult over you with loud singing. (Zephaniah 3:17 ESV)

> Beloved, let us love one another, for love is from God, and whoever loves has been born of God and knows God. Anyone who does not love does not know God, because God is love. (1 John 4:7–8 ESV)

I love that the woman at the dinner party gave it all to the One who gave it all for us.

Just as she poured out her life at Jesus's feet, He in turn poured out His blood for her on the cross. At this point in history, she didn't even know what He would endure for her on the cross, yet she knew He was Lord, and she knew that she needed Him. Because of what Jesus did for her and for all humankind on the cross, we can come to Him in our brokenness and be made whole.

Just as this woman came to Him to receive love and healing, let us come to Jesus and pour out our hearts to Him. He won't heap shame or judgment on us. He loves us and welcomes us. Let this be our reminder to be undone in His presence, praising Him for who He is and worshipping Him as Lord.

Just as she washed the feet of Jesus, He washes us clean and makes us new from the inside out. He poured out His Spirit on us so we can be made clean from our sin and have perfect intimacy with Him—in this life and for all eternity.

Let's end today with this verse:

> He saved us, not because of righteous things we had done, but because of his mercy. He saved us through the washing of rebirth and renewal by the Holy Spirit, whom he poured out on us generously through Jesus Christ our Savior, so that, having been justified by his grace, we might become heirs having the hope of eternal life. (Titus 3:5–7 NIV)

This alone is enough to make us undone.

Questions

1. Read Luke 7:38. Where was the woman standing? What was she doing?
2. Read Titus 3:5–7. How do this woman's actions show us what Jesus does for us?

Day 3: The Fragrance of Faith

I bought a new perfume recently, and when I bought it, I wasn't completely sure about the smell. I knew I needed new perfume, and I was out and about, so I grabbed one. It smelled really strong, but I went ahead and purchased a giant bottle. This is a very "me" move. I often do things in a hurry.

The next day, I sprayed on a generous amount of the new perfume, and when I got into the car, my husband and kids practically choked. My husband doesn't mince words, and he asked me, "Why do you smell like mothballs?" I normally would've been kind of hurt, but I had to agree with him. I smelled awful. I couldn't even stand being in the car with myself!

Lesson learned. Get a sample.

This personal story reminds me of the power of fragrant perfumes—and with that, let's get back to our story.

Read Luke 7:37–38 again.

The alabaster jar this woman brought to the dinner was of great value. Alabaster, which comes from the Greek word *alabastron* meaning "stone casket" or "vase," was considered the best material in which to preserve ointments. Her jar would've been a treasured possession, and it likely cost an entire year's worth of wages.

Let's read more about what the Bible says about perfume:

> I have perfumed my bed with myrrh, aloes and cinnamon. Come, let's drink deep of love till morning; let's enjoy ourselves with love! (Proverbs 7:17–18 NIV)

> While the king was at his table, my perfume spread its fragrance. My beloved is to me a sachet of myrrh resting between my breasts. (Song of Songs 1:12–13 NIV)

These verses give us some context around what she might've used the perfume in her alabaster jar for. We can assume that it would've been a means to her livelihood. She would've used this fragrance to allure lovers into her bed. It was part of her daily profession, so it's interesting that she brought this jar to the dinner party.

A little perfume goes a long way. As this woman wept and poured her entire jar of perfume on the feet of Jesus, the heavy scent would've surely permeated the room. It likely overpowered all the other scents of food and spices, filling the nostrils of every man present. It would've been impossible to ignore what was happening between this woman and Jesus.

Just as a song can take trigger an old memory, certain smells can take your mind to another place. For instance, when I smell a cinnamon candle, I immediately think of Christmas. The smell of freshly baked pumpkin bread reminds me of fall. These smells warm my heart and bring up treasured memories of the holidays and family.

The smell of this perfume would've been a familiar smell to this woman. It was quite possibly the perfume she used in her everyday job, and while the aroma was pleasant, it was also a painful reminder of her sin. Its sweet smell likely added to her tears and brought on great sorrow, shame, and regret.

Pouring out her perfume on Jesus's feet symbolized pouring out her old life of sin. She wept in repentance and worshipped Jesus as Lord. She then took on the fragrance of Christ—the new aroma of faith. The old was gone and the new had come!

> For we are to God the pleasing aroma of Christ among those who are being saved and those who are perishing. To the one we are an aroma that brings death; to the other, an aroma that brings life. (2 Corinthians 2:15–16a NIV)

> Therefore be imitators of God, as beloved children; and walk in love, just as Christ also loved you and gave Himself up for us, an offering and a sacrifice to God as a fragrant aroma. (Ephesians 5:1–2 NASB)

Let's pause for a moment to learn more about aromas and sacrifices in the Bible.

In the Old Testament, God commanded the priests of Israel to continually burn aromatic incense. He instructed them on how to make a recipe of exotic spices to burn on the golden altar inside the holy of holies, the most sacred place in the tabernacle that only the priests could enter to meet with God on behalf of the people.

The aroma burning in the most holy place was pleasing to God, and the Bible says it represented the prayers of His people. Israel was also required to sacrifice certain animals to atone for sin. This was the sacrificial system we learned about in Day 1 that foreshadowed Christ.

> And when he took the scroll, the four living beings and the twenty-four elders fell down before the Lamb. Each one had a harp, and they held gold bowls filled with incense, which are the prayers of God's people. (Revelation 5:8 NLT)

> The Lord said to Moses, "Speak to the Israelites and say to them: 'After you enter the land I am giving you as a home and you present to the Lord food offerings from the herd or the flock, as an aroma pleasing to the Lord—whether burnt offerings or sacrifices, for special vows or freewill offerings or festival offerings.'" (Numbers 15:1–3 NIV)

These verses tell us that the prayers and sacrifices we make to the Lord are a sweet aroma to Him. It pleases the Lord when we pour out our prayers and sins to Him. He loves when we honor Him by offering our time, resources, and lives. These offerings don't go unheard or unnoticed.

The story of the unnamed woman pouring out her alabaster jar on the Lord's feet teaches us that when we pour out our hearts, prayers, sins, and resources to Jesus, the fragrance of our worship fills His nostrils.

Jesus welcomed her and loved her, and He understood what this sacrifice cost her financially, socially, and spiritually. She was pouring out her past and trusting her future to Christ.

Let this be a reminder to us today to pour out our lives at the feet of Jesus as a pleasing aroma to the Lord. It doesn't go unnoticed, and we too can trust Him with our future.

Questions

1. What did the woman bring to the dinner?
2. How much was the jar worth?

3. Read Proverbs 7:17–18 and Song of Songs 1:12–13. Do these verses give you some context around what she might've used this perfume for?

4. Read 2 Corinthians 2:15–16 and Ephesians 5:1–2. How did the woman's sacrifice offer a pleasing aroma to Christ? How does this apply to us?

Day 4: Dos and Don'ts

Sometimes Christians can become so focused on the dos and don'ts of our faith. To be honest, I can get caught up in that works trap too. I can look down on someone or judge a situation just by what I see on the outside. God wants us to put our faith into action, but we should always remember that He cares most about our hearts.

> But the Lord said to Samuel, "Do not consider his appearance or his height, for I have rejected him. The Lord does not look at the things people look at. People look at the outward appearance, but the Lord looks at the heart." (1 Samuel 16:7 NIV)

Simon was completely hung up on the dos and don'ts of religion. He was all about the rules. As we'll see, this self-righteous Pharisee got an up-close-and-personal lesson from Jesus Himself on the dos and don'ts of true faith. He got a taste of his own medicine.

Let's dive in.

> When the Pharisee who had invited him saw this, he said to himself, "If this man were a prophet, he would know who is touching him and what kind of woman she is—that she is a sinner." (Luke 7:39 NIV)

Simon said this in his head, but Jesus heard his thoughts. Don't miss that. He examines the attitudes of our hearts and always knows what we're really thinking.

Simon didn't want the woman to touch Jesus because according to Jewish law then, that would make Him ceremonially unclean. Remember, the word *Pharisee* means "separate." Their whole philosophy was to separate themselves from sinners. They wanted nothing to do with anyone or anything that could make them unclean.

The fact that she was touching Jesus would've been unheard of in this culture, and this situation was getting all over Simon. He was repulsed and saw her only for her sin.

This is also where we see Simon's true motive begin to emerge: His mission was to disprove Jesus as a prophet. I can imagine these thoughts running through his head:

If Jesus were a prophet, He would know that this woman is a sinner.
If Jesus were righteous, He wouldn't let an unclean Gentile woman touch Him.
I can now reject Jesus as a prophet because He clearly doesn't know the rules.

By the way, the Pharisees often questioned Jesus's actions and judged the people He pursued:

> But the Pharisees and the teachers of the law who belonged to their sect complained to his disciples, "Why do you eat and drink with tax collectors and sinners?" (Luke 5:30 NIV)

Simon underestimated Christ. He made a mental list full of assumptions about why He wasn't a prophet or a religious man. Jesus then revealed Simon's heart and turned his thinking upside down.

Read Luke 7:44–48.

At the beginning of the dinner, Jesus was reclining at the table with His back to the woman. In these verses, we see a change in His posture. He directly faces the woman. Jesus turns His back on Simon, the one accusing her, and gives her His undivided attention.

This is such a powerful statement. Jesus's body language displays an acceptance of the woman and a rejection of Simon, her opposer. I love that His eyes never leave her face as He talks to Simon. Jesus is showing her that He's aligning with her and defending her.

He asks Simon our key question this week—"Do you see this woman?"—then goes on to give him a list of what the woman did that he, as the host, didn't do:

You didn't give me any water for my feet.
She wet my feet with her own tears and wiped them with her hair.
You didn't welcome me with a customary kiss.
She hasn't not stopped kissing my feet.
You didn't put oil on my head.
She poured out her greatest treasure before me.

Jesus is letting Simon know that he made several social errors and violated the Jewish law of hospitality. It was customary in that day to greet one another with a kiss, wash guests' feet to clear off the dirt from their sandals, and anoint their heads with oil.

Simon neglected to do all these things. He put little to no effort into honoring Jesus—as if he were too good for Him.

On the other hand, this sinful woman went above and beyond to welcome and worship Jesus. The Bible says that she kissed His feet from the time He entered the party, leading us to believe that she might have arrived early to await His arrival. Her heart was full of love, anticipation, and humility.

I love what Jesus does next: He forgives her sins. This is a lesson we can all apply to our lives.

In His statements, Jesus proved a few things to Simon:

He's more than a prophet.
He has the power to forgive our sin.
He rejects the rules of religion.
He sees right inside the heart.

Let's read more from Jesus on the hypocrisy of judging others:

> Why do you look at the speck of sawdust in your brother's eye and pay no attention to the plank in your own eye? How can you say to your brother, "Let me take the speck out of your eye," when all the time there is a plank in your own eye? You hypocrite, first take the plank out of your own eye, and then you will see clearly to remove the speck from your brother's eye. (Matthew 7:3–5 NIV)

> Blind Pharisee! First clean the inside of the cup and dish, and then the outside also will be clean. (Matthew 23:26 NIV)

Simon was blind to his own need for a savior. When Jesus asked him, "Do you see this woman?" He was essentially saying, "You're standing right here, but you're completely missing what's really going on." Simon was so obsessed with how things appeared on the outside that he neglected to clean "the inside of the cup"—his own heart.

So here's our challenge today: As believers, let's not be defined by hypocrisy or a checklist of religious rules. Let's be known by how much we love Jesus and the people around us.

Questions

1. Read 1 Samuel 16:7. How is God's vision different from man's?
2. What was Simon's motive in asking Jesus to dinner?
3. Read Luke 7:44–48. Who was Jesus facing as He spoke to Simon?
4. What question did Jesus ask Simon? How did He use Simon's theology against him?
5. What did Jesus prove to Simon?

Day 5: Canceled Debt

Well, ladies, we made it to Day 5. I have to admit: I'm sad for this story to end! We can all learn so much from this sinful woman. She's a picture of true worship, true repentance, true thankfulness, and true redemption. Today, we're going to see how she and Jesus wrapped up the party—and how they parted ways.

> Jesus answered him, "Simon, I have something to tell you." "Tell me, teacher," he said. (Luke 7:40 NIV)

I love what Jesus says here. It sounds like what I say to my kids when I've had it. I can hear myself now, with gritted teeth: "Listen up! You have a lecture coming!" My kids know this tone well, and there's normally some eye-rolling on their end.

Jesus goes on to tell Simon a story. He often used stories to help illustrate a moral point.

Read Luke 7:41–47.

Jesus told this story to prove a point to Simon and the woman. This woman was like the man with great debt. Because she was aware of her many sins, she was all the more grateful for Jesus's forgiveness. She understood the meaning of grace because she knew what she had been saved from.

That's where true faith begins. If we can't see our sin, then we'll never see our need for a savior. Jesus always forgives our debt of sin when we come before Him with a repentant heart.

Simon couldn't see his sin. He was too busy judging this woman to realize his own need for a savior. He thought he was clean by his works or outward appearance. He missed the whole point of grace because his pride was in the way.

> I have not come to call the righteous, but sinners to repentance. (Luke 5:32 NIV)

How do we experience this forgiveness in our own lives? Through Jesus alone.

> If we confess our sins, he is faithful and just to forgive us our sins and to cleanse us from all unrighteousness. (1 John 1:9 ESV)

> Let us draw near with a true heart in full assurance of faith, with our hearts sprinkled clean from an evil conscience and our bodies washed with pure water. (Hebrews 10:22 ESV)

> Therefore, if anyone is in Christ, he is a new creation. The old has passed away; behold, the new has come. (2 Corinthians 5:17 ESV)

Jesus cleanses us by His blood. He was the perfect sacrifice for our sins, and when we draw close to Him, bow before Him, and place our faith in Him as Lord of our lives, He washes us clean. We become a new creation! He's the only way to true freedom and forgiveness.

We see this principle play out beautifully in the rest of the story. Jesus acknowledged that this woman had many sins, but also that she had great love for Him. He then warns that whoever has been forgiven little loves little.

What a powerful reminder. As followers of Christ, we should love others, pray for others, and forgive others—just as He forgave us. We love much because we've been forgiven much.

> But because of his great love for us, God, who is rich in mercy, made us alive with Christ even when we were dead in transgressions—it is by grace you have been saved. (Ephesians 2:4–5 NIV)

> A new command I give you: Love one another. As I have loved you, so you must love one another. By this everyone will know that you are my disciples, if you love one another. (John 13:34–35 NIV)

Let's revisit the powerful words Jesus spoke to Simon after telling him the debt story:

> Then he turned toward the woman and said to Simon, "Do you see this woman?" (Luke 7:44a NIV)

Jesus looked at her and called her "woman." Until then, she had been called "sinner." Her shame was her identity, and she carried it with her everywhere she went.

It must've been unnerving for her to hear Jesus call her "woman." I wonder how long it had been since anyone had referred to her that way. Jesus honored her by calling out her true identity: a woman created in the image of God.

> So God created mankind in his own image, in the image of God he created them; male and female he created them. (Genesis 1:27 NIV)

Jesus saw her not for her sin, but for who He made her to be. He was saying, "You are not your sin. I won't label you as others have labeled you."

He then took her from the shadows to the limelight by using her as an example of holiness. He brought positive attention to her by praising her actions in front of the religious leaders who had condemned her. Jesus saw a woman who recognized her sin and poured out all she had at the feet of her Savior. He saw her repentant, worship-filled heart.

Let's see how this story ends.

Read Luke 7:48–50.

Can you imagine what this meant to her? She was weeping at His feet, pouring out her heart, and surely feeling unworthy—and Jesus freed her. He washed her slate clean.

Don't miss Jesus's parting words to this woman: "Your faith has saved you; go in peace."

First, we see that her faith saved her, not her works. It wasn't the dos and don'ts of religion. It was her simple, heartfelt faith.

I also love that He told her to go in peace. She was free to leave her life of sin and move forward. She had been approved by Christ, and all her sin debts had been canceled.

How did the other men at the dinner party react? They said, "Who is this man, that he goes around forgiving sins?"

In forgiving her sins, Jesus both restored this woman's identity and revealed His own. He was more than a prophet. He was—and still is—our Lord.

As we wrap up this week, let's take a moment to celebrate this woman, a true servant of Christ. She fell at His feet, weeping and worshipping. Jesus saw straight into her heart and forgave her many sins. He called her woman and gave her the gift of His salvation, forgiveness, and peace.

This is what Jesus does for us today. When we bring our sin and brokenness to Him and ask for forgiveness, He washes us clean, restores our dignity, and sets us free us to move forward in peace.

Jesus forgives you, saves you, loves you, and sees you. Your debts are canceled.

Questions

1. Read Luke 7:40–47. What's the message behind this parable? How does it apply to the woman at the party?
2. Read Luke 5:32. What do you think this verse means?
3. According to 1 John 1:9 and Hebrews 10:22, how can we experience forgiveness in our own lives?
4. When Jesus called her "woman," how did this speak a new identity into her life?
5. Read Luke 7:48–50. How does Jesus part ways with the woman?
6. According to Jesus's words ("Your faith has saved you; go in peace"), what saved her? How does this go against the Pharisees' theology?

Group Guide

- Open in Prayer

- Watch Week 1 video found at laynietravis.com/doyouseethiswoman (22:43)

- Choose two questions from each day to discuss

- Close in prayer

The Woman Jesus Rescued
(Where Are Your Accusers?)

Day 1: The Trap

This week's story is one of my favorite stories in the Bible. It's about a woman who found herself in a situation she couldn't get out of without divine intervention. It holds loads of drama and the tension is real. This was a life-or-death matter, and once again, Jesus showed us why we love Him so very much. Let's get started.

Read John 8:1–11.

Jesus was totally being set up. This seemed to be a lose-lose situation, but He outsmarted the Pharisees and proved His character.

Have you ever been in a lose-lose situation? Sometimes my kids ask me and my husband loaded questions that set us up to fail. For example, my girls will ask us who we think is the prettiest between them or my boys will ask who we think is the best athlete. These are lose-lose conversations that we never engage in. Playing along and indulging this type of questioning only ever brings about destructive consequences.

Jesus found Himself in a similar situation at the beginning of this passage. He was set up to fail, and His response would determine whether this woman would live or die.

Read John 8:3 again.

The Pharisees and religious teachers put this woman in front of a crowd. She undoubtedly would've felt humiliated, horrified, and utterly exposed, so they obviously had no regard for her feelings. However, this wasn't about the woman. She was just a pawn in their game. This was about Jesus.

Let's not miss that this woman had been caught in the act, meaning that the Pharisees had been watching her. They had been waiting for the perfect opportunity to trap her in her sin.

This reminds of how our spiritual enemy seeks to trap us too:

> Be alert and of sober mind. Your enemy the devil prowls around like a roaring lion looking for someone to devour. (1 Peter 5:8 NIV)

The Pharisees had an agenda: They wanted to trap this woman so they could then trap Jesus. I honestly don't believe that they really cared about this woman's sin as much as they cared about making a fool out of Jesus.

As the story unfolds, they asked Jesus what He thought should happen to her. I can't help but think that when they addressed Him as "Teacher," it was dripping with sarcasm. They were clearly trying to strip Him of this title and make Him look stupid. After all, they prided themselves on being the teachers of the law. They didn't know who they were dealing with.

Remember what we learned in Week 1? God established the law to show the Jewish people how to live in a way that honored Him. Within that law were commandments for marriage to protect both the man and the woman.

> If a man commits adultery with another man's wife—with the wife of his neighbor—both the adulterer and the adulteress are to be put to death. (Leviticus 20:10 NIV)

> If a man is found sleeping with another man's wife, both the man who slept with her and the woman must die. (Deuteronomy 22:22a NIV)

I know these sound harsh, but remember, God is light. In Him, there is no darkness. The law shows us how seriously He takes sin and how serious the consequences are. Thankfully, He sent Jesus to free us from the power and punishment of sin. We can now live under His grace.

The important point here is that under this Old Testament law, both the man and the woman caught in adultery would've been punished the same way because they both participated.

So the fact that the Pharisees brought only the woman shows that they weren't actually upholding the law. They were only accusing the woman.

Shame on them. It takes two to tango.

Knowing this context, let's examine their trap for a moment:

- If Jesus had said that the woman was innocent, they would've accused Him of violating Mosaic law.
- If Jesus had urged them to execute her, they would've said that He contradicted His own teaching of mercy and love for sinners.

The Pharisees were familiar enough with Jesus to have known about the mercy and love He consistently showed to sinners. They were hoping to show that His way of teaching contradicted the law, which said that the consequence of adultery is death. They were trying to prove that Jesus couldn't be both just and merciful.

Here's what the Pharisees failed to understand:

> The Word became flesh and made his dwelling among us. We have seen his glory, the glory of the one and only Son, who came from the Father, full of grace and truth. (John 1:14 NIV)

Jesus is full of grace and truth. He doesn't tolerate sin, but He does make a way for every sinner to be forgiven. He set up the law, then fulfilled it. He showed us the standard of righteousness by living a sinless life, then took the severe punishment our sin requires.

> Jesus answered, "I am the way and the truth and the life. No one comes to the Father except through me." (John 14:6 NIV)

> Then you will know the truth, and the truth will set you free. (John 8:32 NIV)

Jesus isn't just full of truth—He is the truth. When we surrender our lives to Him, He saves us from eternal death and sets us free from the power of sin.

Read John 8:6–7 again.

Boom. Take that, Pharisees.

Jesus's response didn't disrespect the law or excuse this woman's guilt. It simply revealed His grace and His mission: to seek and save the lost.

After all, everyone has sinned. All of us need God's grace. The only one there without sin was Jesus, and He wasn't going to throw any stones. It was as if He was asking them, "Do you hold yourself to the same standard of righteousness you're holding her to?"

Read John 8:9 again.

The Pharisees couldn't outsmart Jesus, so they left. Even when placed in a trap, Jesus proved that He's the personification of grace and truth.

As we like to say in our house, He aced the test.

Questions

1. Read John 8:1–11. What did the Pharisees accuse this woman of doing?
2. Was the venue of this interaction public or private?
3. What was the Pharisees' agenda?
4. Read Leviticus 20:10. According to Mosaic law, who is punished for adultery?
5. How were the Pharisees trying to trap Jesus?
6. Read John 8:6–7. What is Jesus's response to the trap?
7. Read John 8:9. How did the Pharisees respond?

Day 2: The Finger of God

Once a year, we try to do a beach trip with my family. My kids love playing by the ocean, building sand castles, digging for crabs and seashells, and writing their names in the sand. In the story we read yesterday, Jesus also wrote in the sand. Today, we're going to examine what this action symbolized.

Let's pick up where we left off:

> They were trying to trap him into saying something they could use against him,
> but Jesus stooped down and wrote in the dust with his finger. (John 8:6 NLT)

What an odd posture in this heated, drama-filled moment.

Remember, the woman had been thrown out in front of a large crowd where Jesus was teaching. The Pharisees brought her there to try to trap Jesus, asking Him, "What do you say?"

Immediately, Jesus bent down and starting drawing in the sand with His finger. This was no beach. Jesus wasn't playing around. There's purpose in His every move.

So what in the world was He doing? Let's turn to the Old Testament:

> When the Lord finished speaking to Moses on Mount Sinai, he gave him the two
> tablets of the covenant law, the tablets of stone inscribed by the finger of God.
> (Exodus 31:18 NIV)

> Then the Lord delivered to me two tables of stone written with the finger of God,
> and on them were all the words which the Lord had spoken to you on the mountain
> from the midst of the fire in the day of the assembly. (Deuteronomy 9:10 NJKV)

Do you see the pattern? The Ten Commandments given to Moses in the Old Testament represent the original law. Whose finger wrote these laws? God's.

We can put the pieces together now. The Pharisees were hoping to accuse Jesus of not honoring the law, and Jesus began writing in the sand with His finger. He had done this before. As God in the flesh, Jesus had used that same finger to write the law itself. He was demonstrating to the Pharisees that He is justice personified.

Let's read some more verses on what the fingers and hands of God have created:

> When I consider your heavens, the work of your fingers, the moon and the stars, which you have set in place, what is mankind that you are mindful of them, human beings that you care for them? (Psalm 8:3–4 NIV)

> Then the Lord God formed a man from the dust of the ground and breathed into his nostrils the breath of life, and the man became a living being. (Genesis 2:7 NIV)

> But now, O Lord, You are our Father; we are the clay, and you are our potter; we are all the work of your hand. (Isaiah 64:8 ESV)

> But if I cast out demons by the finger of God, then the kingdom of God has come upon you. (Luke 11:20 NIV)

Jesus writing with His finger also symbolized the new covenant of grace He came to bring. At this point in history, His hands were still writing the story.

> For the law of the Spirit of life has set you free in Christ Jesus from the law of sin and death. (Romans 8:2 ESV)

> For the whole law can be summed up in this one command: "Love your neighbor as yourself." (Galatians 5:14 NLT)

Side note: I love that Jesus didn't answer the Pharisees right away, even though they kept demanding an answer. By stooping down to write in the sand, He not only got on the woman's level, but also sent a message that He wasn't going to enter into a theological debate with these religious leaders.

This is a good rule of thumb: Don't get into an argument with a Pharisee. This could be anyone in your life who doesn't want solutions and only wants to win. Jesus didn't try to defend Himself or plead His case—He just kept quiet.

This is hard for me to do. I'm a talker, and I hate when I take the bait and get into an argument that I know will go nowhere. No one walks away better from these types of discussions, so it's often best to just keep quiet.

Ultimately, the Pharisees used their fingers to point out the woman's sin. Jesus quietly used His to point out her path to freedom. The Bible doesn't tell us what exactly Jesus wrote in the sand. Some experts believe that He may have been writing out the sins of the Pharisees present, but no one knows for sure.

What we do know is this: Jesus never once picked up a stone. When He answered the religious leaders that anyone without sin could throw the first stone, He disqualified them all. He was never was going to punish this woman. His plan was to rescue her.

Let's end today with a beautiful promise in scripture. As you read it, think of Jesus rescuing this woman—and think of God speaking this directly to you.

> Fear not, for I am with you; be not dismayed, for I am your God; I will strengthen you,
> I will help you, I will uphold you with my righteous right hand. (Isaiah 41:10 ESV)

The same hands that established the heavens and the earth, formed humankind out of the dust, cast out demons, healed the sick, drew in the sand, and were nailed to a cross are holding you today.

Fear not. You're safe.

Questions

1. Read John 8:6. What did Jesus do as the Pharisees were trying to trap Him?
2. Read Exodus 31:18 and Deuteronomy 9:10. Who wrote the Ten Commandments, and what were they written by?
3. What did Jesus writing in the sand with His finger symbolize?
4. By stooping down to the ground, what else might Jesus have been doing? (Keep in mind that the woman was most likely crouched down, shamefully hiding her nakedness.)

Day 3: Throwing Stones

Throughout the Bible, Jesus is referred to over and over again as a stone. He's called the cornerstone, the stumbling stone, the stone the builders rejected, the stone in Zion, a tested stone, a precious stone, and a stone not cut by human hands.

It's ironic to me that the men in our story this week wanted to throw stones at this woman, all while the stone—the real McCoy—was right there in their midst.

Read Matthew 21:33–46.

In sharing this parable, Jesus was telling the religious leaders that whoever accepted Him would become part of the new nation. They were furious because they realized that the story was about them. I'm seeing a pattern here: Jesus vs. religious leaders = Jesus wins.

At this time, the religious leaders where upholding Jewish law, but rejecting Jesus—the very cornerstone of their faith. Just like the evil farmers who stoned the servants and killed the landowner's son, they refused to open their spiritual eyes and see Jesus for who really He is.

> For no one can lay any foundation other than the one we already have—Jesus Christ. (1 Corinthians 3:11 NLT)

> Therefore, this is what the Sovereign Lord says: "Look! I am placing a foundation stone in Jerusalem, a firm and tested stone. It is a precious cornerstone that is safe to build on. Whoever believes need never be shaken." (Isaiah 28:16 NLT)

> He will keep you safe. But to Israel and Judah he will be a stone that makes people stumble, a rock that makes them fall. And for the people of Jerusalem he will be a trap and a snare. (Isaiah 8:14 NLT)

Like the Pharisees, many will reject Christ as the chief cornerstone, the foundation of the Christian church. Jesus is the rock of salvation for those who believe, but He's also a stone that causes stumbling to those who reject Him. It's an ironic twist that these men wanted to stone the woman caught in adultery, yet in the end, they would be crushed under the stone of Christ.

How does this story apply to us today?

Jesus is our rock. Instead of throwing stones at us, He became the cornerstone for us. He laid down His life so that we can have new life in Him. He also doesn't want us to throw stones at others.

So how do we confront sin without throwing stones?

> Brothers, if anyone is caught in any transgression, you who are spiritual should restore him in a spirit of gentleness. Keep watch on yourself, lest you too be tempted. (Galatians 6:1 ESV)

> Rather, speaking the truth in love, we are to grow up in every way into him who is the head, into Christ from whom the whole body, joined and held together by every joint with which it is equipped, when each part is working properly, makes the body grow so that it builds itself up in love. (Ephesians 4:15–16 ESV)

The Bible teaches us to speak the truth in love, not in judgment. Condemnation heaps shame on others and adds insult to their injury. Our goal should always be restoration, which means getting the person back to Christ and on the road to healing.

We've learned through this story that Jesus separates the sin from the sinner. He doesn't justify sin; He justifies the person. When we come to Him and place our faith in Him, He restores us. He doesn't throw stones at us—He protects us from the stone throwers in our own lives.

Jesus is our chief cornerstone.

Questions

1. Read Matthew 21:33–46. What did the evil farmers do to the landowner's servants and son? How does this relate to this week's story?
2. The Bible refers to Jesus as the cornerstone of the Christian faith. How does this title prove to be ironic in this story?
3. Read Galatians 6:1 and Ephesians 4:15–16. How do we confront sin without "throwing stones"?

Day 4: Woman, Where Are Your Accusers?

I love today's study. We're going to focus on the woman. Can you imagine the trauma she faced? Can you even imagine the shame and embarrassment?

Read John 8:1–3 again.

This woman was not looking for Jesus. She didn't try to earn His approval or seek His attention. The Pharisees forced her into Jesus's path by literally throwing her into His presence.

I can't even imagine being taken half-naked from an intimate act (in the act), dragged across town, and thrust into the presence of Jesus Himself. I get embarrassed going to the grocery store without lipstick on. I mean, I know that God sees everything, but if I was going to officially meet Jesus, I'd want to be in my Sunday best, and I'd probably bring my Bible just to start off on the right foot.

This woman was treated like a piece of property. There she was, stripped of her clothing, dignity, self-worth, and humanity. She was on display for all to see.

This reminds me of something.

> They stripped off Jesus' clothes and put a scarlet robe on him. They made a crown out of thorn branches and placed it on his head, and they put a stick in his right hand. The soldiers knelt down and pretended to worship him. They made fun of him and shouted, "Hey, you king of the Jews!" Then they spit on him. They took the stick from him and beat him on the head with it. (Matthew 27:28–30 CEV)
>
> He was despised and rejected by men, a man of sorrows and acquainted with grief; and as one from whom men hide their faces he was despised, and we esteemed him not. (Isaiah 53:3 ESV)
>
> He was oppressed and afflicted, yet he did not open his mouth; he was led like a lamb to slaughter, and as a sheep before its shearers is silent, so he did not open his mouth. (Isaiah 53:7 NIV)

> This High Priest of ours understands our weaknesses, for he faced all of the same testings we do, yet he did not sin. (Hebrews 4:15 NLT)

Jesus knows our pain. Not long after He rescued this woman, He was put before the crowds, mocked, stripped, mistreated, and despised. He's the high priest who understands.

This woman knew she didn't stand a chance. The Bible doesn't say that she fought her accusers, ran from them, or even yelled back. She didn't utter a word or attempt to defend herself.

My guess is that in her humiliation, she didn't have an ounce of hope left. She just stood there, frozen in fear and dread. She had been ganged up on and bullied into submission.

I hate bullies. I know I appear nice and sweet most of the time, but I have to warn you: I have a streak. My close friends and family know this about me, but if I encounter a bully, something happens, and I can't help but confront him or her. I hate it when someone picks on the weak, and I always cheer for the underdog.

FYI, Jesus does this too.

> What do you think? If a man owns a hundred sheep, and one of them wanders away, will he not leave the ninety-nine on the hills and go to look for the one that wandered off? (Matthew 18:12 NIV)

Jesus always goes after the one who's lost or in danger. He loves the underdogs, the loners, and the vulnerable. He came on a rescue mission for them—for us.

This woman needed to be rescued. Jesus was her only way out. What a picture of redemption! If you also feel trapped in your sin and can't see a way out, know that Jesus is your help in time of trouble. He'll lead you into freedom.

Let's revisit the end of this story by reading John 8:10–11 again.

Jesus stood up again and spoke in posture of authority. He wanted her attention.

This woman's response is the first time we see her speak in this passage. When Jesus asks her if any of her accusers had condemned her, she simply said, "No, Lord." She knew from this interaction that He was her Lord and Savior. I love His response: "Neither do I condemn you."

> What, then, shall we say in response to these things? If God is for us, who can be against us? (Romans 8:31 NIV)

> The Lord is your mighty defender, perfect and just in all his ways; Your God is faithful and true; he does what is right and fair. (Deuteronomy 32:4 GNT)

Jesus doesn't condemn us. He's faithful and true—our mighty defender.

Questions

1. Read John 8:1–3. Where did the Pharisees position this woman?
2. How did the treatment of this woman foreshadow the coming treatment of Christ on the cross?
3. Did the woman attempt to defend herself?
4. Read John 8:10–11. What did Jesus ask the woman? How did He respond to her answer?

Day 5: Go and Sin No More

The road to redemption can be long. It's not easy to change the cycle of our sin, especially sin that's kept us in bondage. Today, we're going to examine the last words Jesus spoke to the woman caught in adultery. What did He mean by them?

Read John 8:10–11 again.

Jesus says, "Go and sin no more" twice in the Bible: to the woman in this week's story and to a man who had been an invalid for thirty-eight years. Jesus miraculously healed the man's condition so he could walk again. Today we're going to examine this story and learn how it applies to us now.

Read John 5:1–15.

Notice the first question Jesus asks the man in this story: "Do you want to get well?" What a profound question. Do we want to get well in the sin-sick areas of our lives?

Jesus asked the man this question before He healed him. He was giving him a choice. Sometimes we can get so stuck in our sin that we don't know another way of doing life. We become miserable, we can't move forward, and we don't really want to take steps toward healing. Freedom from addictive sin is a long road to walk. We have to want to get well.

What does Jesus say to the man after He tells him to "go and sin no more"?

He tells him that if he keeps sinning, something worse will happen to him. Jesus, looking at the man's heart, was warning him that repetitive sin always causes great consequences—both here on earth and in eternity. He was cautioning the man not to fall back into his same sinful patterns.

In the case of the woman in this week's story, her sinful choices clearly contributed to her situation. They got her in serious trouble. The Bible doesn't tell us what this man's sin was or if it contributed to his situation too—but we do know that Jesus let him choose whether or not he wanted to be free.

It's important to note that when Jesus told these two people to "go and sin no more," He wasn't speaking of a lifestyle of perfection. None of us can attain that. He was instructing them to move forward in forgiveness and freedom.

That's His goal for us too. He wants us to live in freedom—without falling back into the bondage of sin. Remember, Jesus is the embodiment of both grace and truth.

This woman wouldn't have been perfect after her encounter with Jesus (none of us are), but she would've definitely been changed forever. I imagine that out of gratitude for the mercy Jesus showed her, she didn't even have a desire to return to the old, sinful life she had before. I can relate to that.

Jesus changes our hearts and our desires. As we pursue Him, we begin to want the things He wants for us. Pastor Craig Groeschel says it like this: "What you feed grows. What you starve dies."

The more we feed on spiritual things, the more our old desires starve. This doesn't mean that it's a quick or easy process. We have to be intentional about leaving our sin behind and pursuing Christ. Whether it's wrong thinking, overeating, lusting, stealing, cheating, an addiction, or any other sin that holds us captive, Jesus tells us to go and leave it behind. It can be a daily grind, but freedom is worth it.

We all struggle in different areas. I know I wrestle with my fair share of sinful patterns, like wrong thinking, losing my temper, pride, gossip, and people pleasing, to name a few. In different seasons, I always seem to be working on a new area of sin that God has brought to my attention. I'm still learning to surrender to the process of restoration, walk close to Jesus, and continually ask for His supernatural help to "go and sin no more."

As we wrap up this week, let's review what we've learned:

Christ is your rescuer. He doesn't see you for your sin. He stands in the gap between you and your accusers to defend and protect you. Most importantly, He came to save you from sin and its power over your life. He came to set you free!

Ask Jesus today to reveal any sin that's holding you captive. Once you've identified it, lay it at His feet, then choose to move forward in freedom.

Go and sin no more.

Questions

1. How many times in the Bible does Jesus instruct someone to "go and sin no more"?
2. Read John 5:1–15. Who else did Jesus say similar words to?
3. What's the first question Jesus asks the man in the story?
4. What does Jesus say to the man after He tells him to "go and sin no more"?
5. When Jesus says, "go and sin no more," is He talking about a life of perfection?

Group Guide

- Open in Prayer

- Watch Week 2 video found at laynietravis.com/doyouseethiswoman (25:49)

- Choose two questions from each day to discuss

- Close in prayer

WEEK 3

The Woman Jesus Healed
(Who Touched My Robe?)

Day 1: Get It Together

The other day, I went to Starbucks to get my afternoon iced coffee pick-me-up. The parking lot is extremely small at this particular location, and I didn't realize that the drive-through was under construction and blocked off until the car in front of me pulled into a parking space. As he was trying to reverse, I pulled forward and accidentally blocked him in. We both ended up trapped. It was a debacle to say the least.

As the other driver got out of his car and approached my window, I rolled down my window, thinking we were going to come up with a plan to get out of this mess. Instead, he yelled in my face, "You need to get it together!" He then turned his back on me and went inside the store.

I was appalled. It was an accident. I didn't dare go inside. I somehow maneuvered my way out of the parking lot and felt so rejected. Now I'm the first to admit I'm not the best driver in the world—but how about a little grace?

This week, we'll explore the story of a woman who was in desperate need of grace herself. She had been physically sick for twelve long years, and due to her condition, the religious leaders considered her unclean. She wasn't allowed to worship in the temple or commune with the people.

We'll also meet a twelve-year-old little girl who was literally at death's door. We'll discover that the desperate woman, the synagogue leader, and the young girl all needed the healing touch of Christ.

This story is told in three different gospels, and I believe that's because God really wants us to get it. We'll read all three accounts to gather all the details and see this story from each perspective.

Read Matthew 9:18–26, Mark 5:21–43, and Luke 8:40–56.

To understand all the rich symbolism and importance of these two miracles, we need to understand more about the characters involved in this story. Let's start with the woman.

Under Jewish law, a woman who was menstruating wasn't permitted to worship until she had completed her cycle. I know this seems like a weird rule. However, about once a month, I may need a break from society due to my mood swings—just saying. This strange law offered women protection and privacy.

> When a woman has a discharge of blood for many days at a time other than her monthly period or has a discharge that continues beyond her period, she will be unclean as long as she has the discharge, just as in the days of her period. (Leviticus 15:25 NIV)

> You must keep the Israelites separate from things that make them unclean, so they will not die in their uncleanness for defiling my dwelling place, which is among them. (Leviticus 15:31 NIV)

According to the religious leaders' interpretation of this law, the woman with the blood disorder was considered permanently unclean. Anything or anyone she touched would've become unclean too. The Bible doesn't tell us specifically which condition she had, but we do know she was unable to worship or be involved in her religious community until it resolved.

Now let's look at Jairus. As the director of the synagogue, he would've been in charge of letting people in and out to worship, learn, and complete their religious duties. As an enforcer of these laws, he would've certainly shooed this woman away from the synagogue anytime she tried to enter. (This reminds me of my Starbucks incident. I can hear Jairus now: "You need to get it together!")

This isolated woman had spent everything she had trying to get well. She had nothing left. When she saw Jesus, she knew that He was her last hope.

> She thought, "If I just touch his clothes, I will be healed." (Mark 5:28 NIV)

> She came up behind him and touched the edge of his cloak, and immediately her bleeding stopped. (Luke 8:44 NIV)

Knowing that she was considered unclean, this woman took the risk of touching the fringe of Jesus's robe. She was hoping in faith that He wouldn't notice, but He did. Even as He was pushing through a crowd of people, Jesus felt the touch of this woman.

Then he said to her, "Daughter, your faith has healed you. Go in peace." (Luke 8:48 NIV)

Don't miss this: This is the only time in the Bible Jesus referred to a woman as "daughter." He did this to show Jairus that she was His daughter too. She was as much of a daughter to Jesus as Jairus's little girl was to him. I don't believe it's a coincidence that Jairus's little girl was twelve and the woman had suffered for twelve years. Jesus was tying these two individuals together.

In Jesus's eyes, this woman wasn't an unclean outcast. She was a daughter of the most-high God, and she was included in God's family. He wanted everyone to see that she and others like her should be allowed to worship. She didn't need to have it all together to come to Jesus. None of us do.

Remember, in the Old Testament, only the high priest who performed rituals to become ceremonially clean could enter into the holy of holies and be exposed to God's presence in the temple. In the New Testament, though, God dwelled among all the people in the person of Jesus Christ. All were welcome in His presence.

By miraculously healing this woman, Jesus showed Jairus that her touch wouldn't make Him unclean. He actually made her clean—a complete reversal and fulfillment of the law.

I can't wait for us to dive more into this story together. For now, take courage, daughter! Know that just like this woman, you don't have to have it all together. Jesus will make you clean.

Questions

1. Read Matthew 9:18–26, Mark 5:21–43, and Luke 8:40–56. Who are the main characters in this story?
2. What disorder does the woman in the story have that keeps her out of the synagogue and ostracized from society? How long had she had this disorder?
3. Why was she exempt from society?
4. What was Jairus's profession, and how old was his sick daughter?
5. According to Mark 5:28, how did this woman believe she could be healed? Was she correct?
6. Read Luke 8:48. What did Jesus call her?
7. By calling her "daughter," what message was Jesus sending to Jairus?

Day 2: Power Exchange

When my sisters and I were little, we had family friends who lived on a cattle ranch. We grew up in the city, so we always loved going to visit their farm. It was like a whole new world with cattle, horses, land, hay, and tractors. It was a kid's dream.

Once while I was playing with our friends in the pasture, they dared me to touch the electric fence. I was around ten and had no idea what would happen, or else I never would've touched it. I accepted the dare, and I remember an electric jolt vibrating through my entire body. I couldn't even open my fingers to let go. I just stood there, shaking violently, until I somehow managed to pry my fingers off the fence.

My friends all died laughing, and I thought I had actually just died. It was horrible! My younger sister Callie, wanting to see what the shock felt like, went on to put her head on the fence—but that's another story for another time.

Today, we're going to see a power exchange sort of like an electric bolt of faith that occurred between Jesus, the woman, and the young girl in our story. As my sister Callie would say, let's dive in head first.

Read Luke 8:43–45 again.

Do you remember where the woman stood in the story of the alabaster perfume we learned about in Week 1? Yes—she stood behind Jesus too. I find it interesting that both of these women intentionally positioned themselves there. They felt so powerless and unworthy of His attention that they didn't even expect Him to see them. Yet, in both stories, He drew attention to them and empowered them.

Gilbert Bilezikian notes that there are several examples in scripture of Jesus reaching out to isolated, unnoticeable women who were viewed as "negligible entities destined to exist on the fringes of life." In each interaction, Jesus sees them and "in one gloriously wrenching moment, He thrusts them on center stage in the drama of redemption with the spotlights of eternity beaming down upon them, and He immortalizes them in sacred history."

Wow. That's so powerful. Jesus not only healed these women, but also gave them influence. He singled them out, drew them out of the shadows of insecurity and shame, and placed them in the spotlight. He gave them a new identity that they could be proud of.

Read Luke 8:45–47 and Mark 5:32–34 again.

Jesus felt the power leave His body. I wonder if it was like an electric shock. Immediately, the woman felt in her body that she had been freed from her suffering. She knew she had been healed. As we read yesterday, Jesus then called her "daughter" and told her to go in peace.

Let's continue on to the second healing in this story.

Read Mark 5:35–42 again.

Jairus's little girl died, and the men at the synagogue told him not to bother Jesus anymore. After all, the worst had happened. Have you ever been there? Maybe you can relate to thinking, *Why bother Jesus now? This situation is hopeless.*

Jesus responds by instructing Jairus, "Don't be afraid; just believe."

Upon arriving at Jairus's home, Jesus found people wailing in grief. When He told them the child was only sleeping, they laughed at Him. But Jesus touched her hand and gave her the power of life. He brought her back from the dead!

So how does this power exchange apply to our lives today?

Know this: Jesus is still in the business of miracles. We can experience His life-changing, miraculous power in our own lives through the Holy Spirit.

> But you will receive power when the Holy Spirit comes on you; and you will be my witnesses in Jerusalem, and in all Judea and Samaria, and to the ends of the earth. (Acts 1:8 NIV)

When we believe Jesus is who He says He is and accept Him as Lord of our lives, He sends us His spirit to live inside us. Just like this little girl received new life, we receive new spiritual life in Christ. The Bible says that we're born again into the family of God.

What do we receive when the Holy Spirit comes upon us?

> The Spirit of God, who raised Jesus from the dead, lives in you. And just as God raised Christ Jesus from the dead, he will give life to your mortal bodies by this same Spirit living within you. (Romans 8:11 NLT)

> But as for me, I am filled with power—with the Spirit of the Lord. I am filled with justice and strength to boldly declare Israel's sin and rebellion. (Micah 3:8 NLT)

Now it is God who makes both us and you stand firm in Christ. He anointed us, set his seal of ownership on us, and put his Spirit in our hearts as a deposit, guaranteeing what is to come. (2 Corinthians 1:21–22 NIV)

After Jesus completed His mission on earth, He poured out the Holy Spirit on all those who accept Him as Lord, giving us eternal life and supernatural power. We now have full access to the spirit of Jesus, which dwells within us.

The Holy Spirit gives us the power to forgive, love, heal, overcome, use our gifts for His glory, be washed clean from sin, and so much more. He always gives us what we need. His miraculous power is limitless.

Through the story of this woman and young girl, we see a glimpse of what happens when God's supernatural power meets our natural circumstances. Like an electric shock, it invades our lives and shakes us up so much that we can't seem to let go. It's a divine power exchange.

Questions

1. Read Luke 8:43–45. Where did the woman stand when she approached Jesus? Does this remind you of another woman?
2. Read Luke 8:45–47 and Mark 5:32–34. How did Jesus realize that someone had touched Him?
3. Read Mark 5:35–42. What happened to Jairus's daughter while Jesus was healing the bleeding woman?
4. What did Jesus say to Jairus when he was about to lose hope?
5. Read Acts 1:8. How do we receive the power of Jesus in our own lives?

Day 3: Loneliness

Let's begin today by reading this verse:

> God sets the lonely in families, he leads out the prisoners with singing. (Psalm 68:6a NIV)

The woman who touched Jesus's robe was certainly lonely. She was isolated from society due to her illness and wasn't allowed to worship or commune in the temple. Anyone she touched would've been considered contaminated. This was the mind-set of all the people she did life with.

This woman was desperate for healing. I wonder if she had been alone in her sickness for twelve long years and didn't have a family to belong to. By addressing her as "daughter," Jesus was letting this woman know that she wasn't alone, that she was His daughter, and that she belonged to His family. Then He restored her back to health so she could reenter society free of her sickness.

The verse we just read also says that God leads the prisoners out with singing. God accomplished both of these principles in this woman: He brought her into His family and released her from the prison of her illness. When she reached out to Jesus, He gave her a new life. She could sing with joy!

This is what Jesus does for us too. When we reach out to Him in prayer and recognize Him as Lord, He hears our prayers, sees us in the crowd, empowers us, frees us, and adopts us into His family.

I love how Nicky Gumbel, an Anglican priest in London, says it: "God does not intend for you to be lonely and isolated. Loneliness has been described as a homesickness for God. God created you for community—calling you into a loving relationship with him and other human beings."

Mother Teresa also said this: "Loneliness and the feeling of being uncared for and unwanted are the greatest poverty."

This woman surely felt lonely, unwanted, and uncared for. She was desperate for community and help.

By calling her "daughter" in all three accounts of this story, Jesus made it clear that she was included in His family. His new covenant is the answer to our loneliness. He wants a personal relationship with each individual person and sends His spirit to dwell within us.

Read Hebrews 8:8–13.

In Christ, we're under a new order that has turned internal. God's law is now written on our hearts, and we're made clean from the inside out. We belong to God and can know Him personally. We can experience His power in our lives, just as this woman did.

Let's look at the healing of the little girl again in this light:

> Then a man named Jairus, a synagogue leader, came and fell at Jesus's feet, pleading with him to come to his house because his only daughter, a girl of about twelve, was dying. (Luke 8:41–42a NIV)

We learn from this verse that Jairus's little girl was his only daughter—possibly even his only child. Jesus not only saved the little girl's life, but He also saved Jairus from the great pain and loneliness of losing his only daughter.

Our God is a personal God. He meets each of us in our unique circumstances and brings His miraculous power. He wants us to live an abundant life. Let's close today with this verse:

> The thief comes only to steal and kill and destroy; I have come that they may have life, and have it to the full. (John 10:10 NIV)

Our spiritual enemy comes to steal, kill, destroy, and isolate us. Jesus came to bring us new life, freedom from eternal death, and fellowship with Him and others. He sets the lonely in families and leads the prisoners out with singing!

Questions

1. Read Psalm 68:6. Where does God place the lonely?

2. By calling this woman "daughter," how did Jesus heal her loneliness? How did He release her from her prison?

3. How does the new covenant that Christ came to bring cure loneliness in our lives?

4. How did Jesus cure Jairus's loneliness in this story?

Day 4: Robes of Righteousness

My friend got me the softest robe ever, and I put it on every morning while I have my coffee. Every day, I look forward to bundling up in it and being warm and cozy. Apparently, Jesus liked wearing robes too. I love that about Him.

Robes are magical, and today we're going to see what they symbolize in the Bible. I might go ahead and put mine back on right now for inspiration.

> Coming up behind Jesus, she touched the fringe of his robe. Immediately, the bleeding stopped. (Luke 8:44 NIV)

> And when the men of that place recognized Jesus, they sent word to all the surrounding country. People brought all their sick to him and begged him to let the sick just touch the edge of his cloak, and all who touched it were healed. (Matthew 14:35–36 NIV)

These are such powerful verses. Just by touching the hem of Jesus's robe, people were healed!

To understand this more, let's learn about the significance of the hem of a robe in Jewish culture.

Read Numbers 15:38–39.

The garment worn by the Israelites in the Old Testament was a long cloth draped over the body. They would attach tassels to the four corners of this garment at the bottom and hem the garment in blue.

The tassels at the hem of the robe served as a reminder that they were to honor God's law, and the colors of the hem symbolized that they were a royal people set apart by God.

Styles changed over time, and instead of having four corners, the garment or robe became more rounded at the bottom. It evolved into a four-cornered shawl called a "tallit" with special tassels, braids, or knots called "tzitzits."

All the religious Jews of this time, including Jesus, wore a tallit with tzitzits hanging off the bottom. So when the woman from this week's story touched the hem of Jesus's robe, she would've touched one of those tassels.

Let's look at some more verses and learn what else this type of robe symbolizes.

Read 1 Samuel 24:1–5.

The corner of someone's robe represented their status and importance. For example, the fringe of Saul's robe would've featured a decorative symbol identifying him as king.

In fact, Jesus once rebuked the Pharisees for enlarging their fringes. The tassels were meant to remind the Pharisees of God's laws, but they used them to magnify their own importance.

> Everything they do is for show. On their arms they wear extra wide prayer boxes with Scripture verses inside, and they wear robes with extra long tassels. (Matthew 23:5 NLT)

In this next verse, the Old Testament prophet Isaiah shares a vision he had of the Lord. Check out what he says about the train of God's robe:

> In the year that King Uzziah died, I saw the Lord, high and exalted, seated on a throne; and the train of his robe filled the temple. (Isaiah 6:1 NIV)

God's robe filled the temple, demonstrating His divine power. He's the King of Kings!

Back to our story. The woman who touched Jesus's garment wasn't just touching a tassel—she was touching His kingship. She was reaching out in faith, believing that Jesus was king and Lord. She was touching the hem of His priesthood, power, and majesty.

Today, we don't have to physically touch Jesus's robe to receive His power. We become wrapped in His robes when we receive Him as Lord and Savior of our lives.

I delight greatly in the Lord; my soul rejoices in my God. For he has clothed me with garments of salvation and arrayed me in a robe of his righteousness. (Isaiah 61:10a NIV)

But you are a chosen people, a royal priesthood, a holy nation, God's special possession, that you may declare the praises of him who called you out of darkness into his wonderful light. (1 Peter 2:9 NIV)

Just as God gave the Jewish people robes to wear as a reminder of His promises, we too are clothed in "robes of righteousness" through His spirit. Let's praise God for robes!

By the way, I just put mine on. Can I get an amen?

Questions

1. Read Matthew 14:35–56. How were people healed in these verses?
2. Read Numbers 15:38–39. What did the tassels on the robes worn by Israelites signify?
3. Read 1 Samuel 24:1–5. Which part of King Saul's robe did David cut off? What did the corner of the robe represent?
4. Read Matthew 23:5. What did Jesus rebuke the Pharisees for regarding their robes?
5. Read Isaiah 6:1. What does this verse say about the train of Jesus's robe?
6. Read Isaiah 61:10. How do the robes of Christ bring us healing power today?

Laynie Travis

Day 5: Take Courage, Daughter

In Christ, we don't have to be afraid. We can rise up and face any person, situation, or circumstance without fear. God is with us.

Let's take a look at Jesus's final words to both the woman and the little girl in this week's story. We'll start with the woman:

> Jesus turned and saw her. "Take courage, daughter," He said, "your faith has healed you." And the woman was cured from that very hour. (Matthew 9:22 BSB)

I love the first part of this verse. We see the posture of Christ reveal His heart yet again. He turned and looked at the woman. She had been invisible, untouchable, and unseen by her community for twelve long years, but Jesus saw her.

After He healed her sickness, Jesus told her to take courage. I love that: He gave her courage, healing, and identity, then told her to take it.

> For the Spirit God gave us does not make us timid, but gives us power, love and self-discipline. (2 Timothy 1:7 NIV)

As believers, we have to take courage too. God's power is there for us. He gives us the Holy Spirit to fill us with faith, love, and holy confidence. We don't have to be afraid.

Now let's take another look at what Jesus said to Jairus, the little girl's father, when he received the news that his daughter had died.

> Overhearing what they said, Jesus told him, "Don't be afraid; just believe." (Mark 5:31 NIV)

Jesus makes it sound so simple. Jairus had just received horrible, earth-shattering, devastating news. Yet Jesus told him not to fear. How does this translate for us?

We don't have to fear any bad news, pending results, diagnosis, or future heartbreak. We just have to believe. Whatever you're facing today, believe that God is good, believe in God's promises, believe that God will provide for you, believe that God will make a way, believe that God will work everything out because He loves you, and believe that God is who He says He is. We can trust Him even in our worst-case scenarios.

> Holding her hand, he said to her, "Talitha koum," which means "Little girl, get up!" And the girl, who was twelve years old, immediately stood up and walked around! They were overwhelmed and totally amazed. (Mark 5:41–42 NLT)

I love that Jesus took the little girl by her hand. It reminds of my kids taking me by the hand when they get afraid while watching a movie like *Star Wars*. It reassures them that I'm right there. Or, when we're crossing the street, I instinctively grab their hands to lead, guide, and protect them.

Jesus took the hand of this lifeless little girl and commanded her to get up. When she opened her eyes, her hand was secure in His. I'm sure He helped pull her up so she could stand.

Life can get us down. It can send us straight to bed, flat on our backs. This little girl was physically dead, but we can be emotionally dead, lifeless, or unable to face life and move forward. We can be taken out by fear, depression, anxiety, and hopelessness.

Jesus taking this child by the hand is a beautiful picture of what He does for us too. When we're paralyzed by fear, knocked flat on our backs, or as good as dead, He takes our hands and tells us to arise! With His power and strength, we can stand up. We can arise to confront that bully, face that situation we've been avoiding, and move forward in faith.

Jesus calls you "daughter" and holds your hand. He won't let you sink. He's right there in the storm with you, commanding you to trust Him and not be afraid.

> Have I not commanded you? Be strong and courageous. Do not be afraid; do not be discouraged, for the Lord your God will be with you wherever you go. (Joshua 1:9 NIV)

Immediately Jesus reached out his hand and caught him. "You of little faith," he said, "why did you doubt?" (Matthew 14:31 NIV)

For I am the Lord your God who takes hold of your right hand and says to you, Do not fear; I will help you. (Isaiah 41:13 NIV)

Get up and take courage! Jesus holds you in His hand.

Questions

1. Read Matthew 9:22. What does the first line in this verse say about the posture of Christ regarding the woman?
2. What did Jesus tell the woman with the bleeding disorder to take? What did Jesus attribute her healing to?
3. How does the line "Take courage, daughter" apply to us today?
4. What did Jesus tell Jairus in Mark 5:31?
5. Read Mark 5:41–42. What did Jesus say to the little girl after He took her hand?

Group Guide

- Open in prayer

- Watch Week 3 Video found at laynietravis.com/doyouseethiswoman (27:06)

- Choose two questions from each day to discuss

- Close in prayer

Week 4

The Woman Jesus Enlightened (Do You Believe This?)

Day 1: Hostess with the Mostest

I love to open my home and host friends and family for holidays, Bible studies, birthday parties, and casual gatherings. However, I also like a clean house. I easily can get into OCD mode and clean like crazy before people come over. Before we have company, my husband, Reese, often finds me on my hands and knees, scrubbing the tile floors with Clorox wipes or cleaning out the pantry.

I've learned to relax over the years, but every now and then, crazy Laynie emerges, and I find myself chasing my kids around the house with a broom to sweep up after their every move.

I'm what you'd call a Type A personality, so I can relate to the woman we're going to study this week. Martha, like me, had some Type A tendencies. She's different from the other women we've studied in that she was considered virtuous. She was a leader in her community and had an honorable reputation—yet just like the other women, her encounter with Jesus left her transformed.

Read Luke 10:38–42.

Martha is mentioned three different times in the New Testament, and in each story, she's accompanied by her sister, Mary. They're a holy pair of sorts in the scriptures. However, they were complete opposites. I have two younger sisters, and we each have completely different personalities too. I think it's interesting how siblings can be related yet wired so differently.

I'm not laid back. I see a goal and go after it, full speed ahead. I've been known to go a hundred miles an hour to finish a project. I often have bumps and bruises from running into things I don't see in an attempt to reach my goal.

All this to say, I can relate to Martha. She was on her feet, cooking, cleaning, working, and making preparations. She had a clear goal in mind, and I admire her action-oriented approach. She would've definitely been someone you could count on to get the job done and do it well. My dad always says, "If you want something done, give it to a busy person."

I think Martha would've been a busy person who took on a lot and enjoyed being productive. The downside of this personality is that it can be easy to miss the blessings right in front of you as you're racing to reach a goal or finish your to-do list.

Laynie Travis

Read Luke 10:38 again.

The text suggests that this home was Martha's. As the homeowner, we can assume that she was responsible for the household affairs. Given that she had the means to own a home and the space to entertain Jesus and His disciples, Martha was likely a prominent figure in her community. She's mentioned in several stories involving Jesus in the Bible.

It's important to note that the first mention of Martha in the Bible is associated with her gift of hospitality. Martha, a virtuous, well-respected woman, welcomed Jesus into her home. This gives us a glimpse into her character. As we've seen, Jesus was rejected by most prominent figures in His day for associating with sinners.

Martha went against the grain. She was a leader who openly supported and loved Jesus.

In the chapter just before He's welcomed into Martha's home, Jesus tells a man that He has no place of rest. The Bible doesn't mention Jesus going back to His home of origin during His three-year ministry. Martha's home is mentioned several times as a place of refuge for Christ. God gave Jesus a gift through Martha's home: a place for Him to refresh and feel welcomed.

> As they were walking along the road, a man said to him, "I will follow you wherever you go." Jesus replied, "Foxes have dens and birds have nests, but the Son of Man has no place to lay his head. (Luke 9:57–58 NIV)

The Bible also tells us that Jesus loved this little family. They were dear friends to Him.

> Now Jesus loved Martha and her sister and Lazarus. (John 11:5 NIV)

Let's get back to the story. Martha invited Jesus and His disciples over for dinner, and in her mind, the pressure was on. She wanted to throw the best dinner party ever—after all, she was entertaining the Son of God! I'd be in a sweeping frenzy.

Notice the question Martha asked Jesus after He and the disciples arrived:

But Martha was distracted by all the preparations that had to be made. She came to him and asked, "Lord, don't you care that my sister has left me to do the work by myself? Tell her to help me!" (Luke 10:40 NIV)

I love this and can definitely relate to her frustration. Here she is killing herself in the kitchen, while her sister, Mary, is sitting at the feet of Jesus. Martha was surely aggravated with her. She most likely wanted to be sitting with Jesus too and found herself thinking, *Thanks a lot, Mary. You've left me to do the dirty work, and you're just sitting there, not lifting a finger!*

I love how she brought her frustration straight to Jesus. She was probably boiling on the inside and started to lose her composure. She was essentially saying, "Look at me, Jesus. I'm over here working myself to death, and you and Mary are having a heyday!" I picture her huffing and puffing in the kitchen, clanging pots and pans around to draw attention and drop some hints.

I think Martha thought Jesus would reprimand Mary for not helping her, but He actually defended Mary. That's so embarrassing, and I have so been there.

Jesus responded by giving Martha a new perspective. We all need His perspective when our thoughts run wild.

> "Martha, Martha," the Lord answered, "you are worried and upset about many things, but few things are needed—or indeed only one. Mary has chosen what is better, and it will not be taken away from her." (Luke 10:41–42 NIV)

Martha sometimes gets a bad rap for her Type A personality, but Jesus loved her, understood her, and enjoyed her. She was gifted in hosting, serving, and getting the job done. So Jesus wasn't saying that serving and preparing aren't good things to do, because they are. He frequently stayed at her home and was blessed by her servant's heart.

What He was saying is that she could choose something better. The gifts Jesus gives us are all good, but we should never choose them over Him. Jesus was gently reminding Martha to choose Him first.

> But seek first the kingdom of God and his righteousness, and all these things will be added to you. (Matthew 6:33 ESV)

Seek Jesus first, and everything else will take its proper place.

Jesus was essentially telling Martha, "The whole point in opening your home was to host me and spend time with me. Here I am, and you're too worried about everything and everyone else."

I think we can all relate to this. When we use our gifts, let's not forget to include Jesus. Our goal should always be to serve Him first. Let's serve Him with joy, let go of perfection, and use our gifts to bless others for His glory.

So the next time I start cleaning myself into an oblivion, snapping at my family, or chasing people with a broom, I'm going to picture Jesus saying to me, "Laynie, Laynie, you're worried and upset about many things. Remember why you're hosting, and don't get caught up in chasing perfection. Choose what's better by putting me first. Everything else will fall into place."

Questions

1. How is Martha's reputation different from the other women we've studied so far?
2. Read Luke 10:38–42. What differences do you see between Martha and Mary? Who do you think is the more laid-back sister?
3. Read Luke 10:38. Who did the home belong to?
4. Why was Martha so mad at her sister Mary? What did she say to Jesus about her feelings?
5. How did Jesus answer her? Why was Mary's choice better?

Day 2: Countercultural

We've learned over the past few weeks that women in Jesus's day were considered second-class citizens. Cultural expectations of women had changed dramatically since Old Testament times.

For instance, in the time of Moses, Jewish women participated in every aspect of community life besides the priesthood. They were free to worship in the temple uninhibited.

However, by the time of Jesus, rigorous religious laws and the influence of pagan cultures had relegated women to seclusion. They were separated from men in private, public, and religious life. A first-century woman's identity came from her ability to bear children and maintain her home.

Jewish rabbis weren't permitted to teach women, and Jewish men weren't even allowed to greet women in public. In fact, one of the prayers of thanksgiving said by Jewish men during this time was "Praise be God that He has not created me a woman."

Jesus, however, didn't comply with these social norms. He shattered these prejudices and showed that women are not second-class citizens in God's eyes. He frequently sought out women who had been ostracized, healed women who were trapped in sin, enlightened women with His teaching, dined at the homes of women like Martha and Mary, and set women free.

Jesus also stepped over human-made boundaries by accepting women as His disciples and including them in His kingdom. He taught them scripture and treated them with respect. He included women in His audiences and specifically taught them profound spiritual truths.

Today we'll see how Jesus revealed this new truth to Martha. Let's review:

> "Martha, Martha," the Lord answered, "you are worried and upset about many things, but few things are needed—or indeed only one. Mary has chosen what is better, and it will not be taken away from her." (Luke 10:41–42 NIV)

To recap, Martha was preparing a meal for Jesus and His disciples, and was frustrated with her sister, Mary, who chose to listen to Jesus's teaching instead. Martha scolded her sister in front of Jesus and demanded that He get her back to the kitchen, where Martha thought she belonged.

Jesus didn't follow her lead. Instead, He taught her a new truth.

By scolding Martha and telling her that Mary had chosen something better, Jesus was letting her know that women have a different role in God's kingdom than they did in her culture. He was teaching her that a woman's place wasn't just confined to the home.

By sitting at Jesus's feet, Mary had taken on the posture of a disciple. Jesus complimented this action and used her as an example to show that women too could be enlightened with spiritual truth. Everyone is welcome to listen and learn at the Lord's feet.

James Hurley says it like this: "The most striking thing about the role of women in the life and teaching of Jesus is the simple fact that they are there. Although the gospel texts contain no special sayings repudiating the view of the day about women, their uniform testimony to the presence of women among the followers of Jesus and to his serious teaching of them constitutes a break with tradition which has been described as being 'without precedent in [then] contemporary Judaism.'"

Women played a prominent role throughout the life and story of Jesus. Over and over in the Bible, we see Jesus seeking women out, teaching them, and giving them a platform in His kingdom. Let's look at a couple of examples.

> Jesus said, "Do not hold on to me, for I haven't yet ascended to the Father. But go find my brothers and tell them, 'I am ascending to my Father and your Father, to my God and your God.'" Mary Magdalene found the disciples and told them, "I have seen the Lord!" Then she gave them his message. (John 20:17–18 NLT)

Jesus appeared first to a woman in His resurrected body, then commissioned her to go and tell His disciples that He had risen—the essential message of Christianity.

Read John 4:21–30.

Jesus revealed the new covenant of His coming Spirit to the Samaritan woman at a well. She was an outcast in her society, yet Jesus sought her out, initiated conversation, and explained salvation to her. He then revealed Himself to her as Lord.

Jesus used her to change her community:

> Many Samaritans from the village believed in Jesus because the woman had said, "He told me everything I ever did!" When they came out to see him, they begged him to stay in their village. So he stayed for two days, long enough for many more to hear his message and believe. Then they said to the woman, "Now we believe, not just because of what you told us, but because we have heard him ourselves. Now we know that he is indeed the Savior of the world." (John 4:39–42 NLT)

Here's what we've learned today: Women have a divine role in Jesus's kingdom. He continually empowered them with His teaching and sent them out to spread His Word. Jesus enlightened Martha with this truth, and He wants to do the same through you.

Questions

1. How did Jesus treat women differently than they were treated by others in their culture?
2. Read Luke 10:41–42. What new perspective did Jesus give Martha that contradicted social norms of the day?
3. What did Mary sitting at a rabbi's feet demonstrate?
4. Read John 20:17–18 and John 4:21–30. What jobs does Jesus give these women?

Day 3: Martha, Martha

When Jesus gently rebukes Martha in this week's story, He affectionately says her name twice. However, this isn't as embarrassing or harsh as it may appear. Today, we're going to see that when the Lord calls a servant's name twice, He has something to say that they need to hear. He has a special calling on their life.

> "Martha, Martha," the Lord answered, "you are worried and upset about many things, but few things are needed—or indeed only one. Mary has chosen what is better, and it will not be taken away from her." (Luke 10:41–42 NIV)

It's very meaningful when God speaks a name twice. Each time a person's name was called out twice in the Bible, that person was elevated to a status of great biblical importance.

Here are a few examples:

- An angel of the Lord called out, "Abraham! Abraham!" as he was about to sacrifice his son Isaac (Genesis 22).
- God said, "Jacob! Jacob!" to tell him to not be afraid to go to Egypt (Genesis 46).
- God called out, "Moses! Moses!" from a burning bush to explain his calling (Exodus 3).
- The Lord called, "Samuel! Samuel!" to give him a message to deliver to his people (1 Samuel 3).

In each of these cases, God wanted to gain the attention of His servant. He had a warning, assignment, encouragement, or gentle rebuke behind the call.

Let's look at what happened through each of these four Old Testament figures:

- Abraham became the father of the Christian faith.
- Jacob, later named Israel, became the nation for God's chosen people.
- Moses became the deliverer of Israel and the prophet through whom God established the law.
- Samuel became first in line of the prophets to bring the messages of God to the people.

All four of these individuals played divine roles in the history of our faith.

In the New Testament, three more key spiritual figures had their names called out twice by God: Peter, Paul, and Martha. Let's examine the times they were addressed this way.

> Simon, Simon, Satan has asked to sift all of you as wheat. But I have prayed for you, Simon, that your faith may not fail. And when you have turned back, strengthen your brothers. (Luke 22:31–32 NIV)

Jesus had a huge job for Simon, also known as Peter. Peter's confession of Christ would be the rock upon which Jesus would build His church.

In these verses, Jesus warns Peter that Satan is going to attack him and try to get him to lose his faith. He also reassures Peter that He had prayed for him and that his faith wouldn't fail. Peter is then commanded to strengthen his brothers in the faith.

Read Acts 9:1–6.

Jesus, speaking from heaven, addressed Saul with a gentle rebuke. This intimate interaction completely transformed Saul's life. He went from killing Christians to becoming known as Paul, the greatest missionary who ever lived and the author of much of the New Testament.

I love how Martha is included with these great men in the double-name references. In her case, the repetition of her name brought an affectionate correction. Jesus lovingly told her to not let her many duties rob her of the blessing of His presence. He wanted her to understand His teaching and prioritize what mattered most.

Let's end today with this promise:

> I have called you by name; you are mine. (Isaiah 43:1b NLT)

Jesus chose Martha for a purpose, just as He's chosen us for a purpose. He calls us by name (sometimes twice) and has a divine calling on each of our lives. We are His.

Questions

1. Read Luke 10:41–42 again. What's the importance of Jesus saying, "Martha, Martha"?
2. Which other Old and New Testament figures were called by God using name repetition?
3. Why is it significant that Jesus placed Martha with these other prominent figures in the faith?

Day 4: If You Had Been Here

Today, we're going to read another story in the Bible involving Martha. I think we'll all be able to relate to the way she wrestles with disappointment—and we'll once again see Jesus enlighten her with a new perspective.

Read John 11:1–44.

Lazarus was the brother of Martha and Mary. They all lived together in Bethany, and they were very close friends with Jesus. He loved them dearly.

When Lazarus became deathly ill, Martha and Mary sent word to Jesus for help: "Lord, the one you love is sick." I love that. We all know the anguish of watching a loved one battle sickness. It's evident in the language the sisters used that they knew Jesus's great affection for Lazarus.

Let's look again at how Jesus responded to Mary and Martha's message:

> When he heard this, Jesus said, "This sickness will not end in death. No, it is for God's glory so that God's Son may be glorified through it." (John 11:4 NIV)

This verse, like many others, holds both a literal and spiritual meaning. Its spiritual meaning is that because of Christ, our physical illnesses won't ultimately end in eternal death. Though our physical bodies will eventually die, our spiritual bodies will live on forever.

> For God so loved the world that he gave his one and only Son, that whoever believes in him shall not perish but have eternal life. (John 3:16 NIV)

At this point in the story, Martha and Mary interpreted Jesus's response literally. They believed that Lazarus wouldn't die physically, so they were naturally devastated when he did. Let's examine their response.

Read John 11:17–20 again.

This is the middle of the story, and it looks bleak. You might be in the middle of a story too. You may have lost hope because it seems like God didn't show up in your situation. Maybe you believed that God would open that door, heal your loved one, give you that promotion, show you what to do, or prevent the worst from happening—but He didn't.

Like Martha, we can often find ourselves asking Jesus, "Where were You? If only You had shown up, things would be different."

When Jesus received the news that Lazarus was sick, He was with His disciples in Jerusalem—less than two miles from Bethany. He could've easily gone there and healed Lazarus immediately. He could've even just said the word and Lazarus would've been healed! But He didn't. Jesus deliberately delayed. It was all part of God's plan.

You know Martha couldn't get her head around this. We've learned that she had a very proactive personality. When she got word that Jesus had finally arrived in Bethany, she took charge and went out to meet Him. She was done waiting around and was ready for answers.

> "Lord," Martha said to Jesus, "if you had been here, my brother would not have died. But I know that even now God will give you whatever you ask." (John 11:21–22 NIV)

I love that she followed her complaint with a statement of trust. She acknowledged Jesus's supernatural power and was still believing for a miracle. Even though her brother had been dead for four days, she understood that anything is possible with Jesus.

In the middle of heartache, loss, bad news, or disappointment, it can sometimes feel like God just isn't there. However, if God chooses to delay or allows something to happen that we don't understand, we can trust that it's always for a greater purpose. Jesus is intentional in His timing.

> Your faithfulness endures to all generations; you have established the earth, and it stands fast. (Psalm 119:90 ESV)

> If we are faithless, he remains faithful—for he cannot deny himself. (2 Timothy 2:13 ESV)

Remember, God's in charge and knows how this is all going to end. His work will be accomplished. Our job as believers is to trust and choose to remain faithful no matter what.

In response to Martha's heartbreak and confusion, Jesus shares with her a new truth that He hadn't revealed to any of His other disciples.

> Jesus told her, "I am the resurrection and the life. Anyone who believes in me will live, even after dying. Everyone who lives in me and believes in me will never ever die. Do you believe this, Martha?" (John 11:25–26 NLT)

In this response, Jesus shared both who He is (the resurrection) and what He brings (eternal life). He revealed His divine nature and told her that death holds no power over Him. Martha thought the resurrection was a future event, but Jesus was showing her that it's a person.

Jesus then personalized these truths to Martha by asking her, "Do you believe this?" He was inviting her into this new knowledge of who He is and what He came to bring.

Here's her answer:

> "Yes, Lord," she told him. "I have always believed you are the Messiah, the Son of God, the one who has come into the world from God." (John 11:27 NLT)

Martha understood who Jesus was: God in the flesh. She was satisfied, comforted, and full of faith, even though she had no idea what was to come.

As we read on in the story, we see that Jesus did bring Lazarus back to life physically. He deliberately waited for Lazarus to die, knowing that He was going to reveal His glory through this miraculous story. If Martha hadn't experienced the great pain of losing her brother, she would've never received these great truths from Jesus.

It's important to note that before Jesus performed this miracle, He wept. He knew that He was going to raise Lazarus from death, yet He still mourned with Martha and Mary first. He understood the depths of their pain.

Jesus is a present-tense God. He loves us in real time. He knows how the story will end, yet He grieves with us in the middle of our pain. He's the high priest who understands, and we can trust Him with our future.

> He will wipe every tear from their eyes, and there will be no more death or sorrow or crying or pain. All these things are gone forever. (Revelation 21:4 NLT)

It's often in our pain, when we're searching desperately for answers, that we're closest to God and hear things from Him that we would've never heard otherwise. When you find yourself in the middle of a painful story, remember to hold on to what we know now. We know that Jesus is Lord, that He's the resurrection and the life, and that nothing is impossible for Him. Let your pain push you to God.

Jesus wants you to believe that He'll work everything out for your good, even when you don't understand. He wants you to know that He's with you and that His timing is perfect.

Do you believe this?

Questions

1. Read John 11:1–44. How did Martha and Mary describe Lazarus to Jesus?
2. In John 11:4, how did Jesus respond to their message?
3. Read John 11:17–20. How long had Lazarus been in the tomb?
4. What did Martha say to Jesus in John 11:21–22?
5. In John 11:25–26, what new truth did Jesus reveal to Martha?

Day 5: Did I Not Tell You?

I'm a smeller. I love to smell things. It's a weird habit that my friends and family often tease me about. I smell everything: my food before I eat it, my hands after petting a dog, my kids to see if they need a bath, and milk—even after it's gone bad. I know, I know. It's so gross, but I'm super sensitive to smells. My husband says I could rely solely on my sense of smell and get through life just fine.

As we finish our story this week, we'll see that Martha and I both get preoccupied with smells. Let's discover what happens when Jesus shows up and does His thing.

Read John 11:38–44 again.

I love Martha. She just can't help being practical.

You can almost hear the exasperation in Jesus's voice as He gives her another lesson. He responds to her smell anxiety by asking, "Did I not tell you that if you believe, you will see the glory of God?"

I love how Jesus asks, "Did I not tell you …?" It's like He was saying, "Remember, I gave you a revolutionary talk. I showed you the keys to salvation and revealed to you who I am—and you're worried about a bad smell?" You know He had to be thinking, *Martha, please quit interrupting and let me do this miracle.*

After they rolled the stone away, Jesus prayed that the people there would know and believe that He had been sent by God. He then called Lazarus out of the grave.

> The dead man came out, his hands and feet wrapped with strips of linen, and a cloth around his face. Jesus said to them, "Take off the grave clothes and let him go." (John 11:44 NIV)

Jesus called Lazarus out of death and into life. He was no longer dead.

This is a beautiful picture of our own salvation. I believe Jesus was giving Martha an illustration of the new truths He had revealed to her. We're all dead in our sins, but Jesus calls us out of the grave by name. When we accept Him as Lord, we hear His voice and follow Him into new life. We replace our burial linens with His robes of righteousness.

This miracle also foreshadowed what Christ would do for us on the cross. At this point in the story, Jesus knew that He would soon be crucified, paying the price for our sins once and for all. On the third day, Jesus's stone would be rolled away, and He too would leave His grave clothes and be raised back to life.

Jesus proved to everyone at the scene of Lazarus's tomb—and again at His own tomb—that He holds resurrection power.

> The angel said to the women, "Do not be afraid, for I know that you are looking for Jesus, who was crucified. He is not here; he has risen, just as he said." (Matthew 28:5–6a NIV)

We can learn a lot from the relationship Jesus shared with Martha. Throughout this week, we've seen Him enlightening her with great spiritual truths. He saw her, understood her, and loved her. He revealed Himself to her as Lord. He demonstrated His great power to her by bringing her brother, Lazarus, back to life!

We can be confident that Jesus knows us and is with us in our pain too. He weeps with us when we suffer and gives us hope for the future.

Let it be our prayer this week to continually be enlightened by Jesus, just as Martha was. Let's choose what's better by putting Him first in our lives and taking on the posture of sitting at His feet. Let's walk daily with Jesus, the resurrection and the life—the God of miracles.

Questions:

1. Read John 11:38–44. What was Martha's reaction when Jesus said to take away the stone?
2. How did Jesus respond to her concern?
3. What happened in John 11:44? What does this event foreshadow?

Group Guide

- Open in Prayer

- Watch Week 4 Video found at laynietravis.com/doyouseethiswoman (24:19)

- Choose two questions from each day to discuss

- Close in prayer

The Woman Jesus Delivered (Shouldn't This Woman Be Set Free?)

Day 1: The Posture of Bondage

My twelve-year-old son, Barrett, is almost as tall as I am. When he was little, he would jump up onto my back and I could easily carry him around. This is no longer the case.

The other day, he playfully jumped on my back, and I literally dropped to my knees under his weight. He was so heavy, I couldn't even move. I yelled, "Barrett, get off my back! You're too big for Mom to carry you like that."

Today, we're going to read about a woman in the Bible who was bent over double and immobile. She couldn't stand up straight under the oppression of her bondage. It was as if she was carrying around a giant preteen! Jesus freed her from this oppressive posture, and she became able to move forward in newfound freedom.

This is a short story, but it's filled with powerful spiritual truths. As we examine it, we'll learn how we too can experience freedom in Jesus. He alone can set us free from anything that keeps us pinned down, immobile, and trapped under the weight of bondage.

Read Luke 13:10–17.

The Bible says that this woman was completely unable to straighten up and that a spirit had kept her crippled for eighteen long years. Let's pause here for a moment.

Can you imagine the agony of this position? This woman's head would've been forced to look only at the ground—a posture of defeat and hopelessness. It would've taken great effort for her to lift her head and socialize with others. Her condition would've caused suffering in every area of her life: physical pain, emotional isolation, frustration, and spiritual discouragement.

Let's dive deeper into the everyday challenges this permanent posture would've brought this woman. For eighteen long years, she would've been forced to stare at the ground and look at people's feet. Since she couldn't straighten her back, it would've been impossible for her to look anyone in the eye. She would've been cut off from human interaction by her posture alone.

It also would've been extremely hard to keep up with conversation. In this limited posture, she wouldn't have been able to read facial expressions or talk with others without them bending down to speak to her or hear her response. I'd bet that over time, she probably lost her voice altogether. What would be the point of talking?

Every moment of her life would've been a struggle. Think about sleeping in this position, getting dressed, bathing, or trying to eat. This sickness would've hindered her entire day-to-day routine.

Finally, remember that in this society, she also would've been considered unclean. Others would've avoided touching her so that they wouldn't become unclean too. She most likely grew accustomed to people turning away to avoid her when she approached them. Rejection would've become part of her identity.

So how does this relate to us? Let's look at a few ways we might find ourselves in this same posture of bondage today:

- Pain: What's the natural posture you take after receiving a gut punch? You most likely bend over, clutching your stomach, and gasping for air.
- Grief: Bad news can feel like an actual punch in the stomach. We can sometimes become so grief-stricken that we can't stand up under the weight of our emotional pain.
- Shame: Have you ever asked an adult a question only to find them studying your feet and afraid to look you in the eye? It's usually because they feel ashamed and insecure.
- Defeat: The players of a losing team often bend over and hang their heads in defeat. We can live out this same posture when we feel beat down or discouraged by life.
- Fear: When facing an enemy or attacker, we might cower down in fear. Fear can cripple us to the point of paralysis where we're unable to stand up and fight back.

We can take on the same posture of pain, defeat, insecurity, shame, fear, and discouragement that this woman had in our own lives. We can even begin to embrace and live out this way of life as our identity.

This woman's posture also gives us a visual picture of the crippling effect of sin that Jesus came to free us from. Here's how King David described it:

> For my iniquities have gone over my head; like a heavy burden, they are too heavy
> for me. (Psalm 38:4 ESV)

Sin weighs a lot. The burden of our lies and shame can hold us down, head to the ground, afraid of being found out. This weight cripples us to the point that we're bent over double and can't move forward in forgiveness and freedom. It torments and oppresses us.

What is oppression? The *Merriam-Webster Dictionary* defines *oppression* as "unjust or cruel exercise of authority or power" and "a sense of being weighed down in body or mind." If we don't take our oppressive sin and emotions to Jesus, they can trap us in the posture of bondage.

The woman in this story gives us a physical picture of what happens when we let the enemy get a foothold in our minds and souls. He wants us to live oppressed and stop pursuing God's purposes for our lives. He's constantly trying to take us out.

> The thief comes only to kill and steal and destroy; I have come that they may have life, and have it to the full. (John 10:10 NIV)

Jesus warns us not to let Satan weigh us down. We need to bring our pain, failures, shame, and sins to Him and let Him set us free.

Let's close today with these words from Jesus:

> The Spirit of the Lord is on me, because he has anointed me to proclaim good news to the poor. He has sent me to proclaim freedom for the prisoners and recovery of sight for the blind, to set the oppressed free, to proclaim the year of the Lord's favor. (Luke 4:18–19 NIV)

Jesus came to set the oppressed free. He came to bring us life!

Questions

1. Read Luke 13:10–17. How did this woman's illness affect her physically and emotionally?
2. Have you taken on a posture of bondage in any areas of your life?
3. How can we experience this kind of posture spiritually?

Day 2: Lighten Your Load

Yesterday, we learned about what a posture of bondage looks like and how we can get stuck in this position ourselves if we're not careful. Today, we're going to see what the posture of a free woman looks like. Let's start with these words from Jesus:

> Come to me, all you who are weary and burdened, and I will give you rest. Take my yoke upon you and learn from me, for I am gentle and humble in heart, and you will find rest for your souls. For my yoke is easy and my burden is light. (Matthew 11:28–30 NIV)

Some of us are so very tired. We're tired of being held down by our sin or shame. We're tired of being oppressed by the lies of the enemy. We're tired of trying to walk with this weight bearing down on our backs.

When we come to Jesus, He gives our weary and burdened souls rest. His yoke is easy. His burden is light. He can set us free.

To understand more of the cultural context behind Jesus's words, let's examine what a yoke is.

A yoke is a wooden crosspiece that's fastened over the necks of two animals, then attached to a plow or cart for them to pull.

Jesus mentioned this common tool of His day to paint a visual picture for the audience. A yoke was often fastened to two oxen so they could share the load of the work. So Jesus was telling us that when we become joined to Him, He shares our burdens and helps us through our trials. When we share the yoke of Christ, our load becomes lighter.

Notice that in the definition of a yoke, there lies a wooden cross. Jesus has already carried the weight of our sin once and for all on the wooden cross. He took our place and died a sinner's death to pay the price for our freedom. He carried the heavy yoke of our sin and shame. He endured sin's crushing weight so we don't have to.

Through these verses, Jesus is telling us, "Come to Me for rest, freedom, forgiveness, and everything else you need. I've already worn your sins on My back. All you have to do is bring Me your burdens, and I'll help you stand up straight. My yoke is easy."

This is how we walk in freedom. We lay our heavy yoke at the feet of Jesus and put on His.

> He personally carried our sins in his body on the cross so that we can be dead to sin and live for what is right. By his wounds you are healed. (1 Peter 2:24 NLT)

> Therefore, there is now no condemnation for those who are in Christ Jesus, because through Christ Jesus the law of the Spirit who gives life has set you free from the law of sin and death. (Romans 8:1–2 NIV)

Let's look again at what happened when the woman in this week's story met Jesus.

> When Jesus saw her, he called her forward and said to her, "Woman, you are set free from your infirmity." (Luke 13:12 NIV)

When Jesus called this woman to Himself, she was still bent over. I can't help but wonder if her situation reminded Him of what was to come: in the very near future, Jesus Himself would be bent over while carrying a wooden cross. He too would be staring at the feet of all who were present, unable to lift His head from the weight He bore.

When Jesus put on the yoke of the cross, He took on her sin, my sin, and the sin of all humanity so we could be set free. When you feel defeated or ashamed, remember this: Jesus already carried the weight of your sin so you don't have to.

> Then he put his hands on her, and immediately she straightened up and praised God. (Luke 13:13 NIV)

Jesus touched this woman, which we've learned was completely against social norms due to the clean/unclean laws of the day. I love that she immediately straightened up. The weight was instantly lifted. It was as if she popped up like a spring that had been held down by a rock.

I know that when I wrestle with shame or regret and confess it to Jesus, I feel an immediate sense of relief. I love the sense of freedom you feel when you get something off your chest or when someone unburdens you from an obligation.

What was the first thing this woman did after she stood up straight? She praised God. I bet she worshipped Jesus like crazy! He gave her a brand-new life. He restored her health, her hope, and her quality of life. She could now took on a new posture of freedom.

> So if the Son sets you free, you will be free indeed. (John 8:36)

I love this verse. It shows us the posture of a free woman. When Jesus sets us free, we're free indeed! We can stand up straight, shake off our burdens, and move forward in freedom. We can also run forward with purpose.

Jesus tells us to run the race, but we can't do that if we're weighed down by the trials of life. A posture of freedom is one that's standing up straight both spiritually and emotionally.

> Let us throw off everything that hinders and the sin that so easily entangles. And let us run with perseverance the race marked out for us, fixing our eyes on Jesus, the pioneer and perfecter of faith. For the joy set before him he endured the cross, scorning its shame, and sat down at the right hand of the throne of God. (Hebrews 12:1b–2 NIV)

Thankfully, we don't carry our crosses alone. We share a yoke with Christ. We're joined to Him, and He lightens our load. We'll certainly face trials and attacks from the evil one, but Jesus has already won the victory. When we take our burdens to Him, He helps us stand up and not get stuck in a posture of defeat. He gives us rest and calls us to freedom.

Jesus died to set us free, so stand up, girls—let's get moving!

Questions

1. Read Matthew 11:28–30. What is a yoke?
2. Read Luke 13:12. What did Jesus say to this woman?
3. How did her posture change?

Day 3: Signs on the Sabbath

Let's pick up today where we left off. The crippled woman met Jesus, and in a word, He set her free. She was healed!

It's no surprise that the Pharisees were irritated about this healing. They became focused not on the miracle itself, but on the rules they felt Jesus kept breaking. He was throwing them for a loop, and they couldn't seem to get a handle on Him.

> Indignant because Jesus had healed on the Sabbath, the synagogue leader said to the people, "There are six days for work. So come and be healed on those days, not on the Sabbath." (Luke 13:14 NIV)

Once again, we see a religious leader of this day getting it all wrong. He was mad at Jesus for setting a crippled woman free on the wrong day. Let's look at the Old Testament to see where this rule came from.

Read Exodus 31:12–17.

When God gave Moses the law, He set the Sabbath apart as a holy day of rest. It served as a sign of the covenant He made with the Israelites and established a new way of life for them. Working on the Sabbath was considered disrespectful to God and brought dire consequences.

While God took the Sabbath very seriously, it was actually a gift to the Israelites, not a punishment. Remember, when they had been enslaved by the Egyptians, they were given no day off. So God gave His people the Sabbath to focus on the necessities of life: rest, worship, and reflection.

Now, fast-forward fifteen hundred years to the time of Jesus. This holy day of rest turned into bondage for the Jewish people. Religious leaders added human-made restrictions to the Sabbath that weren't given by God. They created sixty new columns of regulations that everyone was expected to honor.

These new laws took work to mean anything and everything—not just a break from one's day job. For example, there were detailed restrictions against carrying a burden, which could be earthenware, a piece of paper, animal food, and so on. The general rule was that the people couldn't carry anything heavier than a fig on the Sabbath.

I find it ironic that the Pharisees' burden rules actually ended up creating a great religious burden on all the people. God never intended for this.

Let's see what Jesus had to say about the Sabbath.

> The Lord answered him, "You hypocrites! Doesn't each of you on the Sabbath untie your ox or donkey from the stall and lead it out to give it water? Then should not this woman, a daughter of Abraham, whom Satan has kept bound for eighteen long years, be set free on the Sabbath day from what bound her?" (Luke 13:15–16 NIV)

> He said to them, "If any of you has a sheep and it falls into a pit on the Sabbath, will you not take hold of it and lift it out? How much more valuable is a person than a sheep! Therefore it is lawful to do good on the Sabbath." (Matthew 12:11–12 NIV)

> Then he said to them, "The Sabbath was made for man, not man for the Sabbath. So the Son of Man is Lord even of the Sabbath." (Mark 2:27–28 NIV)

Jesus was furious and challenged the synagogue leader with a question, knowing that his answer would be yes. He called him a hypocrite and a pretender. In contrast, Jesus called the woman "a daughter of Abraham." He was accusing the Pharisees of treating their livestock better than the children of God.

> Jesus replied, "And you experts in the law, woe to you, because you load people down with burdens they can hardly carry, and you yourselves will not lift one finger to help them." (Luke 11:46)

The woman Jesus healed was under great oppression, but so were the people of that day. They didn't have bent backs physically, but they were spiritually loaded down with the weight of rules they couldn't bear. When Jesus set this woman free on the Sabbath, He also set everyone else free.

> Then he added, "Now go and learn the meaning of this Scripture: 'I want you to show mercy, not offer sacrifices.' For I have come to call not those who think they are righteous, but those who know they are sinners." (Matthew 9:13 NLT)

Jesus didn't break the Sabbath by healing this woman; He mercifully brought the Sabbath to her. He released her from the snare of the devil so she could finally rest. God never said not to do good on the Sabbath. He just said to honor it.

I love how the people in the crowd responded:

> When he said all this, all his opponents were humiliated, but the people were delighted with all the wonderful things he was doing. (Luke 13:17 NIV)

Let this be a reminder to us today: God is more concerned with our hearts than with human-made rules. In His mercy, He sets us free and brings us rest. In response, we can worship Him and delight in all the wonderful things He does in our lives.

Questions

1. What's the purpose of the Sabbath?
2. How did the Sabbath change from its original intent?
3. Read Luke 13:14–15. What did Jesus call the synagogue ruler?
4. What did Jesus call the woman?
5. Read Matthew 9:13. What do you think this means?

Day 4: Spirit of Freedom

Today gets interesting. We're going to explore the evil spirit that held the crippled woman in bondage. I know it sounds creepy, but if you're like me, you probably had some questions after reading this story. Let's start by reviewing what scripture says about this woman's condition.

> And a woman was there who had been crippled by a spirit for eighteen years. She was bent over and could not straighten up at all. (Luke 13:11)

The Bible intentionally tells us that this woman had been crippled by an evil spirit. We can assume that this woman wasn't born with her condition and that it wasn't the result of a genetic disposition. Her body was under demonic attack—one that undoubtedly caused inner spiritual torment too. She was suffering physically, emotionally, and spiritually.

> When Jesus saw her, he called her forward and said to her, "Woman, you are set free from your infirmity." (Luke 13:12 NIV)

Jesus didn't say, "You are healed"; He said, "You are set free." This implies that she was in bondage. She was a slave to this condition.

We live in a fallen world, and not all illnesses or diseases have a spiritual root like this woman's did. However, the Bible makes it clear that evil spirits or demons can act as agents of disease and illness. Jesus wants us to be aware that there's a spiritual realm.

> For our struggle is not against flesh and blood, but against the rulers, against the authorities, against the powers of this dark world and against the spiritual forces of evil in the heavenly realms. (Ephesians 6:12 NIV)

Jesus alone can deliver us and protect us from evil forces that try to attack us and take us down. He came to set us free.

> That evening many demon-possessed people were brought to Jesus. He cast out the evil spirits with a simple command, and he healed all the sick. (Matthew 8:16–17 NLT)

Now the Lord is the Spirit, and where the Spirit of the Lord is, there is freedom. (2 Corinthians 3:17 NIV)

And you were also included in Christ when you heard the message of truth, the gospel of your salvation. When you believed, you were marked in him with a seal, the promised Holy Spirit, who is a deposit guaranteeing our inheritance until the redemption of those who are God's possession—to the praise of his glory. (Ephesians 1:13–14 NIV)

Notice the difference between possession and oppression. Once the Holy Spirit is inside us, we're freed from the power of sin and no evil spirit can get in. We become God's possession alone. Nothing else can possess us, but spiritual forces can oppress us.

The enemy will try to get into our minds and oppress us because our actions follow our thoughts. He'll do anything he can to take us out and make us ineffective for God's kingdom. If he can get us to believe his lies, he can get us to live with a mind-set of defeat—one that can actually manifest itself physically.

For example, I once developed Bell's palsy, or paralysis of the face. It was awful! The doctors said that I had developed it due to being in my third trimester of pregnancy, and I know that contributed to it, but at that time, I was battling a lot of anxious thoughts and irrational fears. I believe with all my heart that my mind contributed to my physical health.

God used this condition to teach me that fear was leaving me paralyzed and unable to move forward in freedom. I decided to take the proper medicine prescribed by my doctor, meditate on scripture, and pray that God would renew my mind and bring healing.

I remember surrendering my fears to God and feeling a great spiritual burden lifted from me. Shortly after, my face healed. I still struggle with fear at times, but this story reminds me to trust in God when I feel an attack coming on.

Just as fear affected me physically, other mental lies can manifest themselves as eating disorders, promiscuity, anxiety, and addiction. The devil wants our minds to be held captive.

Let's look now at four ways we can recognize oppression in our lives and stay on the path to freedom.

1. Check your heart. Has anything besides Christ become your master? If you've developed an addiction or obsession—even with something seemingly good, like exercise—that's a good sign that Satan is trying to oppress you.

> "I have the right to do anything," you say—but not everything is beneficial. "I have the right to do anything"—but I will not be mastered by anything. (1 Corinthians 6:12 NIV)

2. Check your motives. Are you making decisions based on fear or faith? Fear is not from God.

> For God gave us a spirit not of fear but of power and love and self-control. (2 Timothy 1:7 ESV)

3. Check your actions. Are you going back to any old self-destructive habits?

> It is for freedom that Christ has set us free. Stand firm, then, and do not let yourselves be burdened again by a yoke of slavery. (Galatians 5:1 NIV)

4. Check your identity. Are you operating out of insecurity or shame? Remember that Jesus loves you and delights in you.

> I praise you because I am fearfully and wonderfully made; your works are wonderful, I know that full well. (Psalm 139:14 NIV)

To fight against spiritual attack, we need to know God's voice, recognize our weak spots, and remember that the Holy Spirit lives within us. When Satan tries to burden us with fear, shame, condemnation, self-hatred, or addiction, we simply need to turn to Jesus. He renews our minds and helps us stand strong in His power.

> Instead, let the Spirit renew your thoughts and attitudes. (Ephesians 4:23 NLT)

We demolish arguments and every pretension that sets itself up against the knowledge of God, and we take captive every thought to make it obedient to Christ. (2 Corinthians 10:5 NIV)

Finally, be strong in the Lord and in his mighty power. Put on the full armor of God, so that you can take your stand against the devil's schemes. (Ephesians 6:10–11 NIV)

Just as Jesus set the crippled woman free, He can release you from any bondage you face. You can live standing straight up, spiritually unburdened by the heavy yoke of slavery. Amen!

Questions

1. Read Luke 13:11. What was the cause of this woman's condition?
2. What did Jesus say to her in Luke 13:12?
3. What does the word "infirmity" mean?
4. What's the difference between oppression and possession?
5. What are four things we can check to recognize oppression in our lives?

Day 5: Praise Jesus

Let's end this week by talking about the freed woman's praise. Sometimes when God answers a prayer in my life, I get so excited that I tell my husband, my mom, and my friends—and I forget to thank God! That's why I love the heart of this woman. We see so much evidence of the condition of her heart as we read between the lines of this story.

For one thing, she was still going to the synagogue despite her condition.

> On a Sabbath Jesus was teaching in one of the synagogues, and a woman was there who had been crippled by a spirit for eighteen years. She was bent over and could not straighten up at all. (Luke 13:10–11 NIV)

After living in this bondage for eighteen long years, she hadn't given up on faith. She was there in the synagogue, listening to Jesus teach. Imagine how hard it would've been for her to go there.

This woman was considered unclean and faced rejection everywhere she went. People would've avoided touching her or sitting close to her, yet she endured emotional and physical pain to go worship. She clearly had a heart for God.

> When Jesus saw her, he called her forward and said to her, "Woman, you are set free from your infirmity." Then he put his hands on her, and immediately she straightened up and praised God. (Luke 10:12–13 NIV)

Jesus called her to Himself and she went. She didn't say no, blame Him for her condition, or walk away. She responded to His call and took the risk of going.

Jesus calls us to come to Him too. He wants us to bring all our bondage and dysfunction to Him so He can make us well and free us up. The first step to freedom is always to go to Jesus.

> Come to me, all you who are weary and burdened, and I will give you rest. (Matthew 11:28 NIV)

Everything and everyone that the Father has given me will come to me, and I won't turn any of them away. (John 6:37 CEV)

When you come to Jesus, He embraces you just as you are. However, He won't leave you there. He always has our freedom in mind.

Then he put his hands on her, and immediately she straightened up and praised God. (Luke 13:13 NIV)

Jesus touched this woman. She would've been starved for affection, and He lovingly accepted her and brought her close to Him. She wasn't being punished by God for her bondage. He wanted to free her.

This is what Jesus wants for you and me. He wants you to come to Him for acceptance, love, and freedom. He wants you to live the life He died to give you!

Notice the first thing the woman did after she straightened up: She praised God. The Bible doesn't say that she jumped up and down, ran around, or even took a single step—it says that she immediately stood up and worshipped God.

Despite her long, horrific, painful journey, this woman didn't hold any bitterness, resentment, fear, or shame. Before she even took her first step as a free woman, she praised God for this miracle. Her heart was so full of gratitude. I want to have a heart of praise like this woman did!

It's easy to lose faith when we face battles in life. We all struggle with different trials, struggles, weaknesses, and infirmities. This world is fallen, and evil exists around us.

However, when we answer Jesus's call to come to Him, we experience His freedom, love, acceptance, and transforming power in our lives. As we wrap up this week, let's take a moment to give Him praise for all the bondage He's delivered us from!

Questions

1. What evidence do we see that this woman never gave up on her faith?
2. Read Luke 13:13. What did Jesus do after He freed her?
3. What was the first thing the woman did after she was healed?

Group Guide

- Open in prayer

- Watch Week 5 Video found at laynietravis.com/doyouseethiswoman (27:19)

- Choose two questions from each day to discuss

- Close in prayer

WEEK 6

The Woman Jesus Comforted (Woman, Why Are You Crying?)

Day 1: Mary Magdalene

Mary Magdalene is a fascinating woman of the Bible. Many of her encounters with Christ are recorded in scripture and embody the themes we've discussed so far. One of the reasons Mary Magdalene's story is so unique is that she walked with Christ intimately as a woman disciple. She played a major role in His earthly ministry.

This week, we're going to learn who Mary Magdalene was and take a close look at two divine encounters she shared with Jesus. We'll learn that Jesus personally revealed profound spiritual truths to her and trusted her to spread the news of His resurrection.

We've seen Jesus change the lives of women throughout this study, and we've learned that we serve a God who sees us, heals us, rescues us, delivers us, and enlightens us. This week, we'll see in Mary's story that we serve a God who also comforts us. We'll see how Christ brought her the ultimate comfort of His presence and revealed Himself as Lord.

Let's begin by learning about who Mary Magdalene was and why she was such a popular woman in the Bible.

Mary Magdalene's name is mentioned many times in the Bible, and each time, she's associated with Jesus and His ministry. After a life-changing encounter with Jesus, she dedicated her life to following Him, supporting Him, and leading others to Him. Mary was a powerful influencer for Jesus, and this week, we'll see how Christ propelled her into her spiritual destiny.

"Mary" was a popular name in Jewish culture. The Bible refers to this Mary as "Mary Magdalene" to associate her with Magdala, the town she came from—a common practice in Jesus's day. For example, Jesus was called "Jesus of Nazareth," Paul was "Saul of Tarsus," and another Mary we studied was called "Mary of Bethany." Magdala was a prosperous fishing town on the western shore of the Sea of Galilee, about three miles from Capernaum.

The Bible gives no record of Mary's marital status, home life, or age, so we can assume that she didn't have any home obligations. This freed her up to follow Jesus from town to town as one of His faithful followers during His three-year earthly ministry.

Mary Magdalene is mentioned fourteen times in the New Testament, and in eight of those, she's associated with a group of women. Her name is almost always first in the list, which tells us that she was a leader among women in the Bible.

> And also some women who had been healed of evil spirits and infirmities: Mary, called Magdalene, from whom seven demons had gone out, and Joanna, the wife of Chuza, Herod's household manager, and Susanna, and many others, who provided for them out of their means. (Luke 8:2–3 ESV)

> Among whom were Mary Magdalene and Mary the mother of James and Joseph and the mother of the sons of Zebedee. (Matthew 27:56 ESV)

> There were also women looking on from a distance, among whom were Mary Magdalene, and Mary the mother of James the younger and of Joses, and Salome. When he was in Galilee, they followed him and ministered to him, and there were also many other women who came up with him to Jerusalem. (Mark 15:40–41 ESV)

Mary Magdalene is also mentioned at the foot of the cross of Christ with two other Marys: Jesus's mother and aunt. This is the only biblical account where her name comes third in the order of women listed, which is appropriate for that scene. The fact that she's even listed with the mother of Jesus shows her closeness to Christ. She was in His inner circle.

> But standing by the cross of Jesus were his mother and his mother's sister, Mary the wife of Clopas, and Mary Magdalene. (John 19:25 ESV)

Mary was there with the mother of Christ, comforting and supporting Jesus to the bitter end. She was completely devoted to Him.

Mary Magdalene is sometimes associated with prostitution or known as a woman of poor repute, but there's no evidence in the Bible that supports these claims.

We do know that she was deeply afflicted by demonic forces before she encountered Christ. Scripture doesn't give us any details of her condition, other than saying that Jesus delivered her from seven demons. He set her free and she was never the same.

> And also some women who had been healed of evil spirits and infirmities: Mary, called Magdalene, from whom seven demons had gone out, and Joanna, the wife of Chuza, Herod's household manager, and Susanna, and many others, who provided for them out of their means. (Luke 8:2–3 ESV)

The Bible says that these women supported Jesus's ministry out of their own means. We can assume that since she's referenced alongside these wealthy, high-profile women, Mary Magdalene most likely had wealth and a position of prominence in her town too. She used her resources to supply for Jesus and His ministry.

All three of the women mentioned—Joanna, Susanna, and Mary Magdalene—were set free from demonic activity by Jesus. Then they fully devoted their lives to Christ and traveled from town to town with Him. I'm sure they each took great risks and endured hardship, rejection, and loss of prestige to follow Christ. Jesus was worth it to them.

Mary Magdalene's first encounter with Christ was life-changing. Jesus saw her and delivered her, but that was just the beginning of her story. In the next few days, we'll see how His presence comforted her and propelled her forward in faith.

This is where our stories begin too. We can experience Jesus's transformational power and forgiveness and respond by giving Him our lives. Jesus sees us and came to bring us salvation, fruitfulness, and freedom from any sins that hold us hostage.

Questions

1. How many times is Mary Magdalene mentioned in the Bible?
2. Read Luke 8:2. How does the Bible say these women supported Jesus's ministry?

Day 2: Deep Waters

We learned yesterday that Mary Magdalene was a powerful influencer for Christ. She had been forgiven and delivered from demonic possession, and as a result, she dedicated her life to following Jesus and ministering with Him from town to town.

We've studied where she came from and how her initial encounter with Christ left her transformed. Today we're going to take a closer look at that encounter.

> And also some women who had been cured of evil spirits and diseases: Mary (called Magdalene) from whom seven demons had come out. (Luke 8:2 NIV)

> When Jesus rose early on the first day of the week, he appeared first to Mary Magdalene, out of whom he had driven seven demons. (Mark 16:9 NIV)

We don't have any specifics on where or when this miracle occurred, but we do know that Jesus cast seven demons out of Mary. Let's examine what this means for her and what it means for us.

In the Bible, seven is a symbolic number that represents completion. The fact that Mary Magdalene had been afflicted by seven demons demonstrates that evil had taken complete control of her. She couldn't escape. She would've been tormented mentally, physically, and emotionally—possibly even driven to insanity.

When Jesus drove these demonic forces out of her, she became spiritually well. He gave her a sound mind and helped her experience true freedom and healing.

Through this miracle, Jesus went deep with Mary—seven demons deep. He healed her completely. It doesn't mean that she was perfect or sinless afterward, but she was completely free from satanic bondage.

Jesus wants to go deep with us too. We all face demons, so to speak, and He wants to restore us to complete freedom. Jesus wants to come in and clean house. We can't be fruitful or productive for His kingdom if we're enslaved to bondage.

For example, you might have some undealt-with baggage from your past that continues to affect your present, or you might operate out of wrong thought patterns that lead you to make bad choices. Maybe you're enslaved to bitterness, which poisons your relationships, or you can't seem to break free from an addiction or unhealthy habit.

I'm not saying you're possessed by demons, but I am saying that anything that keeps us in bondage is not from God. It has evil forces behind it.

> For we wrestle not against flesh and blood, but against principalities, against powers, against the rulers of the darkness of this world, against spiritual wickedness in high places. (Ephesians 6:12 KJV)

On the cross, Jesus freed us from the power of sin and gave us the free gift of eternal life. However, we can be saved and still live enslaved to our demons. In Christ, demonic forces can't possess us or take us over—our souls are completely secure—but they can still torment, oppress, and lie to us. We have to be on guard.

We can do this by going deep with Jesus, just as Mary Magdalene did. She didn't just get her feet wet or dip her toe into spiritual things. She went deep, and as a result, Jesus showed her deep truths and used her as a powerful tool for His kingdom. Her spiritual freedom allowed her to minister and help free others.

Jesus wants to go deep with us too. He wants to bring us to a place of spiritual freedom so we can be fruitful and fulfill our God-given callings. He often told His disciples to go into deep waters, and He wants to go into the deep places of our hearts too.

> When he had finished speaking, he said to Simon, "Put out into deep water, and let down the nets for a catch." (Luke 5:4 NIV)

> The purposes of a person's heart are deep waters, but one who has insight draws them out. (Proverbs 20:5 NIV)

As we go deep by studying God's Word, praying, and pursuing Jesus, He brings His spirit into our lives—and where the Spirit is, there is freedom and healing.

> Now the Lord is the Spirit, and where the Spirit of the Lord is, there is freedom. (2 Corinthians 3:17 NIV)

> For the one whom God has sent speaks the words of God, for God gives the Spirit without limit. (John 3:34 NIV)

We can have as much of the Holy Spirit as we want. There's always more with God. As we seek Jesus and meditate on His truths, He'll pour out His spirit into our lives until we overflow, bringing life to everyone around us. That's how we go deep.

Let's look at one more example of going deep—this time from the prophet Ezekiel in the Old Testament.

Read Ezekiel 47:1–12.

God showed Ezekiel a temple that had water pouring out from under its porch. At first, the water only covered Ezekiel's ankles, but as it grew, it became knee-deep, waist-deep, and eventually deep enough to swim in. It was pure and purified everything it touched.

This is a powerful picture of our lives. God says that our bodies are temples of the Holy Spirit, which washes us clean and saves us. We're ankle-deep in His kingdom. As we seek Jesus more and more in our everyday lives, He pours more of His spirit into our hearts and minds.

His Spirit brings healing and freedom that overflows to reach others around us. We become a river of living water that produces fruit and blesses others. We become influencers for the Kingdom, just like Mary Magdalene.

> Whoever believes in me, as Scripture has said, rivers of living water will flow from within them. (John 7:38 NIV)

The deeper we go with Christ, the more freedom we experience—and the more influence we have for Him. Let Jesus go deep with you today.

Questions

1. Read Mark 16:9 and Luke 8:2. How many demons was Mary freed from?
2. Why is the number seven significant? What does this mean?
3. Read Luke 5:4 and Proverbs 20:5. What does it mean to "go deep"?
4. Read 2 Corinthians 3:17. What does the Spirit of the Lord bring?
5. Read Ezekiel 47:1–5. What does this picture represent?

Day 3: Dry Your Tears

I love today's study. We've learned about the great depth of Mary Magdalene's relationship with Jesus, and now we're going to examine a powerful exchange they shared at His tomb after He rose from death. Jesus revealed Himself to Mary in His resurrected body and brought her the supernatural comfort of His presence.

Read John 20:1–18.

Mary Magdalene went to the tomb of Christ heartbroken. She had just witnessed the horrors of the cross. She had stood by Jesus during the final hours of His life and offered emotional support to bring her master some sort of comfort in His horrific agony.

> Many women were there, watching from a distance. They had followed Jesus from
> Galilee to care for his needs. Among them were Mary Magdalene, Mary the mother
> of James and Joseph, and the mother of Zebedee's sons. (Matthew 27:55–56 NIV)

Mary witnessed all the events surrounding the crucifixion. She would've heard the mock trial where Pontius Pilate announced Jesus's death sentence. She would've seen the crowds chanting, "Crucify Him!" She would've witnessed the abuse hurled at Jesus and seen His humiliation as His clothes were torn from His body and a crown of thorns was pushed deep into His skull. She would've seen the beatings He took, the cross He had to carry, the nails driven into His hands, and the suffering He bore.

She was there for it all. Fear didn't stop her from openly supporting Jesus with her presence, and He knew she was there.

I believe that Mary Magdalene's faithfulness contributed to Christ's decision to appear to her first after His body had been resurrected from death. Just as her presence had comforted Christ, He in turn comforted her with His presence. Mary was given the honor of seeing Jesus in His resurrected body before anyone else even knew He was alive—including the twelve disciples. It was an intimate, intentional revelation.

> Early on the first day of the week, while it was still dark, Mary Magdalene went
> to the tomb and saw that the stone had been removed from the entrance. (John
> 20:1 NIV)

> Then the disciples went back to where they were staying. Now Mary stood outside
> the tomb crying. As she wept, she bent over to look into the tomb and saw two
> angels in white, seated where Jesus' body had been, one at the head and the other
> at the foot. They asked her, "Woman, why are you crying?" (John 20:10–13 NIV)

Mary was the first to notice that the stone had been removed. After the disciples left, she had been
outside the tomb crying. When she entered, two angels asked her our key question for this week:
"Woman, why are you crying?"

Let's look again at how Mary responded to them:

> "They have taken my Lord away," she said, "and I don't know where they have put
> him." (John 20:13b NIV)

Mary's response to the angels reveals the depth of her feelings. You can hear the desperation in her
voice. It's as if she was asking them, "Where did they put Him? Where did He go? How will my
life go on without Him? What now?" Her hope was shattered.

> At this, she turned around and saw Jesus standing there, but she did not realize
> that it was Jesus. He asked her, "Woman, why are you crying? Who is it you are
> looking for?" Thinking he was the gardener, she said, "Sir, if you have carried him
> away, tell me where you have put him, and I will get him." (John 20:14–15 NIV)

We can assume by Jesus's question—the same question the angels asked—that Mary had never
stopped sobbing. She was communicating through tears. Have you ever been there? Have you ever
been so wrought with grief that you just couldn't stop your tears?

I know that one of my kids is really hurt or upset when they can't seem to take a breath between
their sobs. They communicate with a shaky, breathless voice, trying to control their tears long
enough to say what's upsetting them. Moms, you know this kind of cry. It demands immediate

attention. I hold them tight, tell them to take a breath, and try to calm them until they can gain their composure.

This is the state of grief Mary was in. I love that Jesus asked her the question, "Woman, why are you crying?" I picture Him holding her face in His hands and tenderly looking into her tear-filled eyes. He was about to tell her the best news and turn her tears of sorrow into tears of joy.

Mary had seen her Lord and deliverer being crucified. She was grieving not only His horrific death, but also the loss of His presence in her life. Jesus had set her free and given her new life, and now He was gone. She had lost everything and was in desperate need of comfort.

Like Mary, we've all experienced the pain of death. Maybe you've walked through the death of a loved one, the death of a dream, the death of hope, or the death of a marriage.

> Jesus wept. (John 11:35 NIV)

Remember, it wasn't that long before His crucifixion that Jesus wept over the death of His dear friend Lazarus. He understands the pain death brings.

Jesus's question to Mary—"Woman, why are you crying?"—also carries a greater scope of meaning. Notice that He calls her "woman," not "Mary." I believe He wasn't just asking her this question, but all of us. We don't have to grieve without hope because Jesus defeated sin and death on the cross. Death is not final.

> O death, where is your victory? O death, where is your sting? (1 Corinthians 15:55 NLT)

> Brothers and sisters, we do not want you to be uninformed about those who sleep in death, so that you do not grieve like the rest of mankind, who have no hope. For we believe that Jesus died and rose again, and so we believe that God will bring with Jesus those who have fallen asleep in him. (1 Thessalonians 4:13 NIV)

Jesus knew why Mary was crying. She was mourning His physical death, the death of His ministry, the death of her hope, the death of her newfound faith, and the death of His presence in her life. He appeared to her and revealed that He wasn't dead.

> Jesus said to her, "Mary." She turned toward him and cried out in Aramaic, "Rabboni!" (which means "Teacher"). (John 20:16 NIV)

Jesus called Mary by name and gave her the gift of seeing Him face-to-face. She heard His familiar voice and knew right away that it was Him. He then revealed a new truth to her: He's alive. Death in any form has no hold on Him.

This scene also gives us as believers a picture of what's to come. In this life, we have the comfort of Jesus's supernatural presence. One day, though, we'll see Jesus face-to-face, just as Mary did. He'll hold our faces in His hands and wipe away our tears once and for all.

> He will wipe every tear from their eyes, and there will be no more death or sorrow or crying or pain. All these things are gone forever. (Revelation 21:4 NLT)

> And behold, I am with you always, to the end of the age. (Matthew 28:20b ESV)

Jesus's presence was very much alive in Mary Magdalene's life, and it still is in ours. He's with us. He's Immanuel—"God with Us." No matter what death we face, this life isn't the end.

Hear Jesus asking you today, "Woman, why are you crying?" Bring Him your tears. Let the comfort of His presence bring you peace, and let the hope of the future bring you joy.

Questions

1. Read John 20:1–18. Who first saw that the stone had been rolled away from the tomb of Christ?
2. In John 20:11, what was Mary doing outside the tomb?
3. Who did Jesus first appear to in His resurrected body?
4. What question did Jesus ask Mary? What greater question do you think Jesus is asking?
5. In John 20:16, how did Mary respond?

Day 4: The Seeker

I've always had a curious nature. I'm what you might call a seeker. I like to gather information, and I'm always asking my husband lots of questions. I love hearing about every detail of his day: who he talked to, what they thought, what they said, and on and on. We joke often because his stories never include enough details to satisfy my curious mind. Reese will often tease me and say, "Curiosity killed the cat."

I'm also a seeker in my spiritual life. The Bible fascinates me, and I love learning about Jesus. I have an unquenchable hunger for more knowledge of Him.

We'll learn today that Mary Magdalene was a seeker too. She was relentless in her search for Jesus. We saw evidence of her passionate pursuit in the story we read yesterday, and we're going to continue exploring that same story today. We'll take a closer look at the second question Jesus asked Mary: "Who is it you are looking for?"

> Ask and it will be given to you; seek and you will find; knock and the door will be opened to you. (Matthew 7:7 NIV)

Jesus wants us to seek Him, and He welcomes our questions. I find great comfort in this. (I keep Him busy with all of mine!)

This is exactly what Mary did. Yesterday, we learned that after the other disciples had left, she remained outside the tomb crying. She wasn't ready to leave because she hadn't found what she had been looking for. She was desperate for answers.

Curiosity got the best of her, and she bent down to look inside the tomb. She continued seeking. Even though she didn't know where Jesus was or what was to come, she kept looking for Him—and in her search, she found exactly who she was looking for.

So how do we seek God in our own lives? We seek Him with intentionality. We seek Him with determination. We wait patiently for Him.

Mary was determined to find Jesus's body. She went to the tomb, asked questions, and waited. The other disciples went home, but she waited. This gives us a picture of a true seeker. In our own lives, we need to be this relentless in our search for Jesus by reading His Word daily, praying at all times about everything, and waiting patiently for Him to move on our behalf.

God is always there, but He wants a mutual relationship with us. He desires a reciprocating love relationship that takes effort on our part as well. As we seek Him, His will, His direction, His presence, His peace, His love, His gifts, His wisdom, and His forgiveness in our lives, He promises that we'll find Him. He longs to reveal Himself to us.

> At this, she turned around and saw Jesus standing there, but she did not realize that it was Jesus. (John 20:14 NIV)

> The Lord your God goes with you; he will never leave you nor forsake you. (Deuteronomy 31:6b NIV)

Jesus is in every situation, even if we don't see Him right away. There will be times when we wonder, "Where is God in this?" We may not see how God is working or feel like He's even there. However, scripture tells us He never leaves us or forsakes us.

Let's look again at how Mary responded to Christ:

> Thinking he was the gardener, she said, "Sir, if you have carried him away, tell me where you have put him, and I will get him." (John 20:15b NIV)

She was determined to find Him. I love how Jesus revealed Himself to her:

> Jesus said to her, "Mary." She turned toward him and cried out in Aramaic, "Rabboni!" (which means "Teacher"). (John 20:16 NIV)

This exchange not only shows us that Jesus is a personal God, but also reveals the nature of their relationship. She was a student and learner, forever seeking answers from her teacher, Jesus.

Here's the lesson for us: We're not always going to understand. More often than not, we won't. However, Jesus assures us that He's with us and He'll reveal His glory in our lives if we don't give up.

Let's ask ourselves the question Jesus asked Mary: "Who is it you are looking for?" Are we seeking Jesus? Or are we seeking attention, fame, fortune, love, security, or popularity?

In our lives, we'll often search for answers, especially if you're of a curious nature like me. In that search for love, meaning, and hope, we'll always come up short if we try to find fulfillment in anything or anyone but Jesus.

He's the answer. He's the truth. He's the only way to true satisfaction and true life.

> Jesus answered, "I am the way and the truth and the life. No one comes to the Father except through me." (John 14:6 NIV)

Let's be seekers, just as Mary was. She knew who she was looking for, and she found Him. As we wrap up our study, take a moment right now to meditate on these scriptures:

> Look to the Lord and his strength; seek his face always. (1 Chronicles 16:11 NIV)

> God did this so that they would seek him and perhaps reach out for him and find him, though he is not far from any one of us. (Acts 17:27 NIV)

> And without faith it is impossible to please God, because anyone who comes to him must believe that he exists and that he rewards those who earnestly seek him. (Hebrews 11:6 NIV)

> You will seek me and find me when you seek me with all your heart. (Jeremiah 29:11 NIV)

> Those who know your name trust in you, for you, Lord, have never forsaken those who seek you. (Psalm 9:10)

Never stop seeking Jesus. You'll find Him.

Questions

1. Read John 20:15. What's the second question Jesus asked Mary?
2. How would you define the word "seek"?
3. Who are you seeking?
4. How can we seek God in our own lives?

Day 5: I Have Seen the Lord!

As believers, we have the assurance that Jesus is with us and that His presence never leaves us. There are those times, though, when He reveals Himself to us in such a way that we just have to exclaim, "I have seen the Lord!"

That's exactly what Mary Magdalene did when Jesus appeared to her after rising from death. She saw her Lord! I pray that like Mary and the other women we've studied the past six weeks, we can claim this in our own lives too. Jesus sees us, and He wants us to see Him in return.

Today we're going to finish the story in John 20 and see what Jesus commissioned Mary to do. Let's dive in.

> Jesus said to her, "Mary." She turned toward him and cried out in Aramaic, "Rabboni!" (which means "Teacher"). Jesus said, "Do not hold on to me, for I have not yet ascended to the Father. Go instead to my brothers and tell them, 'I am ascending to my Father and your Father, to my God and your God.'" (John 20:16–17 NIV)

Jesus appeared to Mary before anyone else—even His twelve disciples. What an honor for this woman with a past to be chosen as the first person to see His risen body! She also received the first assignment given by Christ in the new covenant: to go and tell the others what she had seen.

Remember the story in Week 4 of the Samaritan woman at the well? After her encounter with Christ, she also went and told others what Jesus had done for her. Her testimony brought many people from her community to Christ.

> The woman left her water jar beside the well and ran back to the village, telling everyone, "Come and see a man who told me everything I ever did! Could he possibly be the Messiah?" So the people came streaming from the village to see him. (John 4:28–30 NLT)

> Many Samaritans from the village believed in Jesus because the woman had said, "He told me everything I ever did!" When they came out to see him, they begged

him to stay in their village. So he stayed for two days, long enough for many more to hear his message and believe. Then they said to the woman, "Now we believe, not just because of what you told us, but because we have heard him ourselves. Now we know that he is indeed the Savior of the world." (John 4:39–42 NLT)

Jesus met the Samaritan woman alone at a well. He sought her out, saw into her soul, and gave her the keys to eternal life. When she inquired about a coming savior, Jesus told her, "I am the Messiah!" He revealed Himself to her as Lord, just as He later did to Mary Magdalene.

The Samaritan woman then ran and spread the good news throughout her village. She didn't feel condemnation from His knowledge of her, but freedom. Jesus saw her, and in return, she saw Him.

Let's compare the Samaritan woman's story with Mary Magdalene's. She too heard the Lord and was obedient to His instructions. She went and told the rest of the disciples what she had experienced.

> Mary Magdalene went to the disciples with the news: "I have seen the Lord!" And she told them that he had said these things to her. (John 20:18 NIV)

Both Mary Magdalene and the Samaritan woman shared their encounters, and as a result, they brought others to Christ.

Jesus reveals Himself to us not just for our benefit, but for others' as well. He doesn't want us to just cling to Him for our own comfort. We're eyewitnesses of His power and shouldn't keep it to ourselves. We go and share the good news of Christ so others can come to know Him too. There's so much power in our personal testimonies.

> For we did not follow cleverly devised tales when we made known to you the power and coming of our Lord Jesus Christ, but we were eyewitnesses of His majesty. (2 Peter 1:16 NASB)

> We couldn't be more sure of what we saw and heard—God's glory, God's voice. (2 Peter 1:19a MSG)

> But you will receive power when the Holy Spirit comes on you; and you will be my witnesses in Jerusalem, and in all Judea and Samaria, and to the ends of the earth. (Acts 1:8 NIV)

The disciples experienced Christ so powerfully that they couldn't help but go and tell. Jesus reveals Himself to us in such a way that we can't help but spread the news of our faith to others.

I love what Mary said to the disciples after her encounter with the living God: "I have seen the Lord!" This bold proclamation wraps up this study perfectly. In Week 1, we began with Jesus asking the Pharisee, "Do you see this woman?" Now Mary brings this question full circle by courageously sharing her faith in Christ.

Each of the women we've studied shared an intimate, face-to-face encounter with Jesus that left them completely transformed. He saw them, rescued them, healed them, enlightened them, delivered them, and comforted them with His presence. Like Mary Magdalene, each of them could boldly exclaim, "I have seen the Lord!"

Jesus changes us and makes us new. He's a personal, life-giving God and desires a personal relationship with you. He sees us, knows us intimately, and loves us unconditionally. He rescues us from our accusers, delivers us from bondage, heals the broken places of our souls, enlightens us by renewing our minds, imparts spiritual truth to us, comforts us with His everlasting presence, and ultimately reveals Himself as Lord of our lives. When we meet Christ personally, He radically transforms us.

Whoever you are and wherever you are, Jesus wants you to know that He sees you. The God who sees you wants you to see Him too. He wants to hear you proclaim, "I have seen the Lord!"

Questions

1. Read John 20:16–18. What did Jesus tell Mary to go do?
2. What did Mary say to the disciples?
3. Where in your life have you also "seen the Lord"?
4. Skim John 4:3–42. What did the Samaritan woman say in verse 39?
5. What did Jesus commission both of these women to do? How does this apply to us?

Group Guide

- Open in prayer

- Watch Week 6 Video found at laynietravis.com/doyouseethiswoman (27:11)

- Choose two questions from each day to discuss

- Close in prayer

Printed in the United States
By Bookmasters